girlfriendship

WHITAKER
HOUSE

deepercalling

GIRLFRIENDSHIP

ISBN-10: 0-88368-807-7
ISBN-13: 978-0-88368-807-6
Printed in the United States of America
Australia: © 2004 by Mary Simpson & Alyson Passauer
United States of America: © 2005 by Mary Simpson & Alyson Passauer

Artwork & Design by Belinda McCullough, Bam Graphic Design
Photography by Amanda Spurling (where noted)

31 Girl Ministries
e-mail: marys@ccc.org.au

ɯ
WHITAKER
HOUSE

1030 Hunt Valley Circle
New Kensington, PA 15068
website: www.whitakerhouse.com

(deepercalling
www.deepercalling.com

Library of Congress Cataloging-in-Publication Data

Simpson, Mary 1970–
Girlfriendship / by Mary Simpson and Alyson Passauer.
p. cm.
Summary: "A collection of real-life stories, photography, advice columns, and tips for
girls in their teens"—Provided by publisher.
Includes bibliographical references.
ISBN-13: 978-0-88368-807-6 (trade pbk. : alk. paper)
ISBN-10: 0-88368-807-7 (trade pbk. : alk. paper)
1. Teenage girls—Religious life. 2. Female friendship—Religious aspects—Christianity.
I. Passauer, Alyson, 1975– II. Title.
BV4551.3.S57 2005
248.8'33—dc22
2004028286

1 2 3 4 5 6 7 8 9 10 ɯ 11 10 09 08 07 06 05

mary
For my beautiful nieces–
Alisha, Aimee, Esther, and Jordy-Belle
May your lives be filled with the priceless
memories of lifelong friendships

by Amanda Spurlin

alyson

For my favorite girls—
my beautiful mother, Evelyn, and my little
princess, Jordan

by Amanda Spurling

Contents

foreword by
christine pringle

Having read Mary's stunning debut book *31 Girl*, I was delighted when the invitation to write the foreword for *girlfriendship* was presented to me. Just writing the word *girlfriend* brings a smile to my soul, for I have been blessed with a full cup of amazing friends who make my life complete.

Some time ago, a book titled *Divine Secrets of the Ya-Ya Sisterhood* came into my hands. It was the extraordinary story of the "Ya-Ya's," four diverse women bound by their unfailing friendship. One critic declared, "Every woman should have her own pack of Ya-Ya's," to which I cried, "Oh, I do, I do!" My Ya-Ya's are Heli, Bernie, and Jules respectively.

I so name them, not in the order of my affection (for I love them all), but in the order of their divinely timed entrances into my life. I believe the power of friendship to influence and shape our lives is as great as the influence of a spouse.

I first met Heli in the '70s in New Zealand. She was quiet and shy. I was not! I loved Heli's sweet spirit and still do. She was the calm woman I wasn't. She was (and is!) Valium to my mad world. We have grown up together and raised our kids side by side. We have prayed, fasted, wept, and rejoiced through the years. She ministers without fuss—that's my Heli.

Enter Bernie, the tiny blond bride. It was the summer of 1980. From the moment we met, we "clicked." For the nine years she lived with her family in New York, our friendship remained fast. Bernie has been my left brain, and she reads my heart accurately. Her strength of spirit and tidy mind (you should see her cupboards!) have given me great joy. She interprets my spontaneous ideas and makes them work!

Then, in dances (literally) Jules. She is the "Tahitian Princess" in my group of Ya-Ya's. With glossy raven hair, Jules is forever etched in my mind when I think of our early years, sitting by the pool poised for more fun! With a heart of gold, Jules completes my intimate circle of "girlfriendship."

With us, the chemistry is right!

Now, as a woman of fifty, with the years of building such rewarding friendships firmly planted in the heart of who I am today, I think of you, the next generation, and how vital your choice of girlfriends will be in shaping your destiny. I pray you truly find your very own forever Ya-Ya girlfriends, friends who will sharpen your life and do you good—friends who will strengthen you when you are weak, visit you when you are sick, love you when you are being plain ugly, and stand up on your 30th, 40th, and 50th birthdays to sing "Happy Birthday"!

Above all, I pray you live wonderful lives together, as we have, "keep walking" together, as we have, and embrace your children's children together—as we have! So, it is with great joy that I commend this beautiful book to you. I know you will be inspired to create and nurture "girlfriendships"—as Mary and Alyson creatively show and tell you how!

Love,
Chris
PASTOR CHRISTINE PRINGLE
SENIOR MINISTER
CHRISTIAN CITY CHURCH OXFORD FALLS

P.S. I am delighted to say that, in 2004, Mary joined our staff at Christian City Church Oxford Falls and my group of girlfriends. She works around the corner from me and, like Bernie, she is immaculately tidy! (Help! I'm surrounded!)

mary's thank-yous

Jesus. You are my Savior, my Shepherd, and my Passion. You are what my life is all about.

Wayne. After almost two decades together I still can't believe how much I love just hanging out with you. You are my best friend and greatest encouragement. Let's always keep loving, dreaming, and believing together.

Jake (my little Afro Boy). I can't imagine my life without you and am eternally grateful that I was chosen to be your mom.

My parents. Thank you for teaching me to love God, love life, and love people.

Pastors Philip and Heather. My dreams came true in your house. Thank you for believing in me, loving me, and allowing me to flourish.

Pastors Phil & Chris and Mark & Bernie. Thank you for welcoming me with open arms and open hearts. I look forward to serving you in the greatest place on earth—the beautiful House of God.

Aly & Marcus. It was a privilege and a pleasure to pass the baton to you both. Wayne and I love you guys and thank you for your unwavering loyalty, amazing support, and the type of friendship that others only dream about.

alyson's thank-yous

God. You are amazing, and I love You with everything in me.

Mom & Dad. You are my heroes, my friends, my greatest teachers. Thank you for teaching me to fly, and for making coming home so irresistible!

Philip and Heather. It is my privilege to be part of your team. Thank you for your leadership, friendship, and overwhelming belief in me. I am eternally grateful.

The Staff and Leaders of Riverview Y&YA Ministry. You define unity, passion, strength, and commitment. Thank you for giving hope to a generation.

Riverview Youth and Young Adults. You are all beautiful, each incredible—amazing beyond words.

Mary. I am utterly convinced that we were born to be friends. You and Wayne are so precious to us. We are overwhelmed with love and gratitude toward you both.

To Princess Jordy. I see the world through your eyes, and I can't help but love it!

To my gorgeous husband, Marcus. I love you beyond measure. You are my strength. Let's dream the impossible together. Let's live extraordinary lives together. Let's grow old gracefully together. Let's be in love for eternity.

mary & alyson's thank-yous

To the *girlfriendship* Girls. Thank you for allowing us into your secret places and for sharing your hearts so honestly, so brilliantly. We are so proud of and in awe of you.

Amanda Spurling. Once again, you have captured everything that is beautiful in our girls. Thank you for your patience, your creativity, your passion, and your friendship.

Belinda McCullough. You are a graphic design superstar! Thank you for making this book come alive with your creative brilliance.

I shot an arrow into the air,
It fell to earth, I knew not where;
For, so swiftly it flew, the sight
Could not follow it in its flight.

I breathed a song into the air,
It fell to earth, I knew not where;
For who has sight so keen and strong
That it can follow the flight of song?

Long, long afterward, in an oak
I found the arrow, still unbroke;
And the song, from beginning to end,
I found again in the heart of a friend.

HENRY WADSWORTH LONGFELLOW

girlfriendship

introduction:
born to be friends

"Each friend represents a world in us, a world possibly not born until they arrive, and it is only by this meeting that a new world is born."
ANAIS NIN

by Amanda Spurling

Born to be friends

I'll never forget the first time I met Aly.

I had been invited to a friend's 21st birthday party, and Aly had been asked to give a speech in celebration of this milestone.

Now, usually when you're asked to give a speech at someone's birthday party, you assume that it needs to be poignant, funny, moving, and possibly no more than five minutes. And on recollection, it was funny, moving, and slightly poignant, but after half an hour of hearing this girl waffle on, it was utterly mind-numbing! (In fact, I think Aly spoke for at least 45 minutes!)

And that really sums up my first few experiences with Aly. She was this miniature windup, nonstop, talking gadget. I thought she was ditzy, dizzy, annoyingly girly, and totally nutty!

In fact, there was no way it even crossed my mind that this girl would end up being my best friend. I couldn't imagine that, over the years, she would be the one I shared my deepest joys and disappointments with; that she would pretend to be my sister so she could be the first visitor to see my newborn son in the hospital; that I would be willing to be woken up at 3:00 a.m. to comfort her when she was homesick. I couldn't imagine that I would be able to come to her defense when people lied about her; to cry, console, and pray with her a thousand times over; to celebrate her engagement; to experience the joy of being her matron of honor at her spring wedding and, eighteen months later, to be introduced as "Aunty Mary" to her beautiful baby girl!

I used to hear people say that God has a sense of humor, and now I know it's true. It's hilarious to think that He would set up two totally opposite people to meet and become the best of friends. And I think that's the case with many great friendships. They just don't make sense! You can't work them out in your mind; you just have to experience them with your heart. And when you look back over the years and reminisce about these friendships, you feel incredibly blessed, amazingly loved, and unquestionably secure in the knowledge that someone knows the real you.

This is the magical world of girlfriendships. Friendships that color our lives with laughter, fun, love, and hope, and bonds that are strengthened by shared disappointments, hurts, tears, and loss. They are unique, irreplaceable, and one-of-a-kind friendships that create a new world within us.

Girlfriendship is all about the importance of girl-to-girl friendships. Although many of you reading this book may someday have a boyfriend or husband (if you don't already), there is something so irresistibly special about having great girlfriends who understand us and care about us. In fact, I have an amazing husband (he is seriously too good to be true), but nothing compares to having a friend who is not only a girl (yeah!) but also from the same planet as me and speaks my lingo!

This book has been written to help you develop these friendships and recognize the common pitfalls that threaten relationships between girls. Each chapter also has a story written by a girl just like you and an advice column to lend a hand as you maneuver through this unique ride of life called *girlfriendship.*

So here's to you, beautiful friend. Here's to the exquisitely orchestrated friendships that you were created to experience and the girlfriends you were destined to make memories with.

Here's to your divine girlfriendship journey ahead...savor it!

only know, the vague companionship that I'd seen grow so imperceptibly, turned gold, and ran in tune with all I'd thought, or dared to plan. I don't remember when I first began to call you "friend." One day, I only know, the vague companionship that I'd seen grow so imperceptibly, turned gold, and ran in tune with all I'd thought, or dared to plan. I don't remember when I first began to call you "friend." One day, I only know, the vague companionship that I'd seen grow so imperceptibly, turned gold, and ran in tune with all I'd thought, or dared to plan. I don't remember when I first began to call you "friend." One day, I only know, the vague companionship that I'd seen grow so imperceptibly, turned gold, and ran in tune with all I'd thought, or dared to plan. I don't remember when I first began to call you "friend." One day, I only know, the vague companionship that I'd seen grow so imperceptibly, turned gold, and ran in tune with all I'd thought, or dared to plan. I don't remember when I first began to call you "friend." One day, I only know, the vague companionship that I'd seen grow so imperceptibly, turned gold, and ran in tune with all I'd thought, or dared to plan. I don't remember when I first began to call you "friend." One day, I only know, the vague companionship that I'd seen grow so imperceptibly, turned gold, and ran in tune with all I'd thought, or dared to plan. I don't remember when I first began to call you "friend." One day, I only know, the vague companionship that I'd seen grow so imperceptibly, turned gold, and ran in tune with all I'd thought, or dared to plan. I don't remember when I first began to call you "friend." One day, I only know, the vague companionship that I'd seen grow so imperceptibly, turned gold, and ran in tune with all I'd thought, or dared to plan. I don't remember when I first began to call you "friend." One day, I only know, the vague

girlfriendship

chapter 1: jackpot!
how to win the friendship lottery

"I don't remember when I first began to call you 'friend.' One day, I only know, the vague companionship that I'd seen grow so imperceptibly, turned gold, and ran in tune with all I'd thought, or dared to plan."

FLORENCE STEIGERWALT

Jackpot!
how to win the friendship lottery

It happened on a Monday. I remember the day so clearly. I remember spending the weekend wishing Monday morning would never come. But it did. A bright and sunny March morning.

Birds chirped and bantered playfully at my bedroom window. The alarm clock radio filled the air with the latest hits on the morning show. The neighbor's kids called excitedly to one another as they filled the minutes between breakfast and the school bus with a new backyard adventure. Even the dog seemed to be smiling.

I felt insulted. Could the universe have been any more insensitive? Hadn't God informed the world that I was having a bad case of Monday-itis and, therefore, could everyone please be considerably less jovial in my presence? The sun's bright rays, the cloudless sky, the chirping birds—all seemed to be mocking me, laughing defiantly at my black mood.

As I grabbed my car keys, sunglasses on my head, I couldn't help but wonder what the day would bring. Mary and I worked together; it wasn't like we could avoid each other. As I headed toward the office, I wondered silently to myself how things had gotten so weird. There was such a heaviness in my heart, such confusion and despair. Why was I feeling so down? Why had I let her get to me so much? Why did I care what she thought anyway? It's not like we shared some special bond. It's not like I owed her anything. It's not like she was my best friend....I hardly knew her, for goodness sake.

"Then why are you so upset?" The words pierced my heart. I recognized the voice immediately. It was the voice of my conscience, the voice of my spirit rising up above the murky depths of my discontent. As I pulled into the parking lot and turned off the engine, tears began to sting my eyes. My voice quivered with emotion as I whispered to myself, "I don't know why it hurts so much, it just does."

I will never forget that day. It was the day, six years ago, that I realized Mary Simpson was fast becoming my best friend. It was a revelation I had never expected. Mary had asked me to meet her that day for a heart-to-heart chat about why I was acting so strangely toward her. Truth was, she scared me. Mary was not afraid to challenge me. She knew me so well and that made me feel incredibly vulnerable. I didn't want to get close to her.

So many of my experiences of friendship with other girls had become dramatic disappointments, and I truly wasn't ready for another. I fiercely guarded my privacy and completely distrusted any new players who showed up on the friendship scene. I had spent the first few years of my twenties without many female friends, and in all honesty, I had grown accustomed to being alone. While I didn't always enjoy it, I was comfortable being "Miss Independent."

But Mary was different. She got me. She understood what I really meant when I said stuff that was vague or attitudinal or sarcastic. She wasn't afraid to challenge my thinking and make me evaluate my actions. At the same time, I both loved and hated that someone in my life could have that sort of knowledge about me without my express permission.

That day, Mary and I sat and talked for almost two hours. We talked candidly about our emerging friendship. We talked honestly about our hopes, disappointments, and fears. That day, we made a pact, a promise that we have kept regardless of how much it costs us. And yes, it has cost us at times.

We made a decision to be there for one another like only girlfriends can. We promised that we would encourage each other and speak well of each other. We pledged that we would celebrate each other's "glory moments" and that we would be there for each other in times of disappointment and sorrow. I don't think we could have ever realized how these promises would impact our lives.

That March day, I found a sister I never knew I had. A girl who had the decency to look me in the eye and express her concerns for me without an ulterior motive. A friend who, having seen me at my worst, still wanted heaven's best for me.

Sometimes opening yourself up to a new friendship can be terrifying. But sometimes, just sometimes, it brings to life the most ingenious of God's plans for us—the genuine, unconditional love and resounding grace of a true friend.

As I left the office and drove home, the birds were still chirping and the sun was still shining. As I turned onto my street, the neighbors' kids were out playing, this time climbing a huge tree in their front yard.

"It's been a glorious day, hasn't it?" Their mommy smiled at me.

"Yeah, it has. Perfect." I smiled back.

A **best friend**
is a **sister**
destiny forgot
to give you.
UNKNOWN

advice column

Q: Help! I have never had a best friend. I'm very shy and find it quite difficult to make friends. I have known most of my friends since I started high school, and although I like these girls, I couldn't say that any of them are my best friends. Sometimes I feel lonely because I don't have anyone to talk to. I would really love to make new friends and become a better friend but don't know where to begin. Can you help me?

A: Your problem is similar to that of so many girls we speak with. You have many friends, girls you know well, but none of them stands out as being the one you really connect with. As girls, we love the idea of having that extraordinary friendship that no other friendship compares to—the kind where we feel a kindred bond, where we are not just friends but soul sisters.

I wish I could give you a quick-fix solution to your problem. But the thing about girlfriendships is that they take time to develop. They evolve and become deeper the more we invest in them. In fact, most of the best friendships I know were not necessarily formed because two girls had a goal to become best friends but because, in sharing their lives, that was the natural result.

Although you may not have one particular best friend, it sounds like you are blessed to have a number of girlfriends with whom you have shared many years, and it is entirely possible that you may develop a special bond of friendship with one or two of these girls as you grow older together.

The truth is that many girls do not have one particular best friend, and sometimes we place a little too much importance on finding that one extraordinary friendship. My niece is in high school and has many great girlfriends, but none of these is a closer or "better" friend than the others. She cherishes all the girls in her friendship group as each enriches her life in a different way. You may find that your situation is similar and that each of your school friends will bring a different aspect of friendship to your life.

So don't be anxious! Treat your girlfriends with love and respect, and they will love you for it. Maybe you can talk to some of the girls you feel closest to about how you feel. You might be surprised that they do understand and may even feel like you do at times.

Also, it takes courage to look outside your normal circles and befriend someone else. Are there other girls outside of your normal friendship group who you like talking to or hanging out with? Be daring! Make a decision to get to know these girls. Invite them over for a movie night, or throw a pajama party and invite both your old friends and some new girls. Most of all, make the effort to be friendly and to smile. No one can resist another human being who seems genuinely interested in her. Shyness is something many of us have to learn to overcome, and though it may take some practice, you will love the rewards of your newly found courage!

Cheraine's Story

While thinking about friends, a few very special girls come to mind, five of whom are very close to my heart, each of them unique and special in her own way.

The first two of these girls I met when I was just eight years old, on my first day at Yidarra Catholic Primary, the school where I would spend the next four years of my life.

I was a nervous, shy child, very conscious of being the new student in a big and different environment. The principal was a kind gentleman. He was showing me my new classroom when two high-spirited, fresh-faced young girls popped up from behind him. One of these girls, Ashleigh, had a sweet smile and short brown hair, and I took an instant liking to her. The other girl also had a smile that lit up her face and rather strange, frizzy blond locks. Her name was Zuzanna, and I found my shyness melting away when I returned her smile.

The three of us became inseparable, and having these friends was truly a blessing to me. I had gone through a rough two years prior to that because of my parents being transferred. I had changed schools four times in the past two years, and in all of these schools I had never made any real friends. I had been teased for various things, including my dyslexia, and had as low a self-esteem as an eight-year-old could possibly have.

Ashleigh, Zuzanna, and I happily continued the journey of elementary school together, and I look back on those days as possibly the most idyllic in my life so far. I was in a great school, my teachers were wonderful, and most of all, I had the two most wonderful friends in the world—my dreams seemed to have all come true. When we graduated from elementary school, we promised to stay close during high school. Ashleigh and I even imagined our lives beyond high school, making plans to get a job at the same place and work together. We just knew nothing would ever separate the three of us.

On the first day at Corpus Christi College, our new high school, we were separated into three different classes. Our school was divided into four different houses. Zuzanna and I were at least in the same house, Bateman, which was red, but Ashleigh was in Forrest, which was gold. Most activities were done in our houses, so we rarely did anything with Ashleigh. Not being together really shattered us, and I missed having my friends in the same classroom as me, as they had been for the past four years. I saw Zuzanna occasionally, when we would join with the other red homeroom, but I rarely saw Ashleigh, and to this day, it saddens me that our friendship is not as close as it once was. We knew high school would be different, but this was a huge change.

There were some positives that came from being separated, though. It meant I would have to branch out and find other friends, and in my search to find a friend, I came across a quiet, reserved girl who was in my Design Technology class. Her name was Jaqueline, and in a class full of boys, we felt lost, so I was glad we met each other. Jaqueline and I built up a very strong friendship and could always help solve each other's problems.

Later on that year, I met two more girls from my own house. I was put into a group to work on a project with Veronica and Sarah, two of the smartest girls in my class. I wondered if I would fit in with such brilliant girls. However, Veronica and Sarah welcomed me with open arms and taught me so much. We found we communicated exceptionally well about the project and also found that we talked for hours about other things close to our hearts. This sparked a wonderful and lasting friendship, and I really can't imagine what it would have been like without these two in my life. They are the best, most genuine friends anyone could ask for.

I have gone through so much and done so much with all my friends this year, especially with Sarah and Veronica. We have become as close as sisters, and although we only met a year ago, I feel like we have known each other all our lives.

Sure, sometimes we have our rough times, but so does every healthy friendship, and we never let that worry us too much because we know our friendship is too strong to be broken by little things that come and go.

Over my last two years in high school, I have also formed other special friendships with some very special people. There are too many of these lovely people to name, but I treasure their friendships just the same.

Last night I was at Sarah's place for a Christmas party with all my close friends. Everyone was in high spirits, and over the noise and chattering, I said a silent prayer of thanks to God for one of the best blessings He could have ever given me...a group of great, awesome, generous, and fantastic friends!

girlfriendship

ee, but in the hearts of true friends. Remember, the grea
ift is not found in a store nor under a tree, but in the hear
ue friends. Remember, the greatest gift is not found in a s
or under a tree, but in the hearts of true friends. Remem
he greatest gift is not found in a store nor under a tree, b
he hearts of true friends. Remember, the greatest gift is
ound in a store nor under a tree, but in the hearts of true frie
emember, the greatest gift is not found in a store nor und
ee, but in the hearts of true friends. Remember, the grea
ift is not found in a store nor under a tree, but in the heart
ue friends. Remember, the greatest gift is not found in a s
or under a tree, but in the hearts of true friends. Remem
he greatest gift is not found in a store nor under a tree, b
he hearts of true friends. Remember, the greatest gift is
ound in a store nor under a tree, but in the hearts of true frie
emember, the greatest gift is not found in a store nor und
ee, but in the hearts of true friends. Remember, the grea
ift is not found in a store nor under a tree, but in the heart
ue friends. Remember, the greatest gift is not found in a s
or under a tree, but in the hearts of true friends. Remem
he greatest gift is not found in a store nor under a tree, bu
he hearts of true friends. Remember, the greatest gift is
ound in a store nor under a tree, but in the hearts of true frie
emember, the greatest gift is not found in a store nor und
ee, but in the hearts of true friends. Remember, the grea
ft is not found in a store nor under a tree, but in the heart
ue friends. Remember, the greatest gift is not found in a

chapter 2: telling it like it is

communicating the hard truth

"Remember, the greatest gift is not found in a store nor under a tree, but in the hearts of true friends."

CINDY LEW

Telling it like it is
communicating the hard truth

One of my best friends in high school was a girl named Meredith.

She was a real individual who didn't really care what others thought about her. She was even considered a little eccentric. But that's what I loved most about her, and we had the best times together.

One of the eccentric little habits we faithfully followed was scrutinizing each other's appearance so we wouldn't embarrass ourselves. We'd pretend to casually smile, and then check each other's teeth to make sure no leftover lunch bits were protruding from our teeth. We'd say, "How's my nose?" which was cryptic code language for "Are there any evil nasal nasties hanging out?" And most importantly, we'd ensure that our skirts weren't tucked into our underwear after coming out of the bathroom.

We never wanted to be one of those poor souls who had no one to tell them that their fly was open or that they had toilet paper happily waving to everyone from under their skirt.

Meredith and I pledged an oath that if either one of us was in an embarrassing situation, looked embarrassing, or was simply being an embarrassment, then we would tell each other...no matter what!

And when I look back on my friendship with Meredith, I think it would be great if we all had friends who would tell us the hard truth about ourselves. Friends who look out for us, not only when we have spinach stuck in our teeth, but also when we're oblivious to being stuck in the green goo of life.

So many of us have blind spots in our lives, things we do that we're blissfully ignorant of but that are eye-openingly obvious to everyone around us.

Some of those blind spots are just plain annoying, such as biting our nails or playing with our hair. But other blind spots are more serious. These are emotional blind spots such as moodiness, rudeness, and oversensitivity, or physical blind spots such as dependence upon harmful substances and unhealthy eating habits. If left unchecked, these blind spots will be stumbling blocks to our dreams and will sabotage our futures. I remember vividly when I had to raise one of these serious blind spots with Aly.

I noticed that Aly was regularly unwell. She suffered from migraines and was low on energy. She would call in sick at work and get tired easily. At the same time, I noticed she wasn't eating well. She skipped meals, rarely had breakfast, and basically had poor eating habits. It wasn't very hard for me to put two and two together and realize that her unhealthy eating habits were contributing to her poor health.

So one day I said to her, "Aly, we need to talk."

We went out to a nearby park and over the next couple of hours, I shared with her my concern over her health. In sharing my concern with her, I didn't say it in an "I'm-so healthy-and-you're-an-anemic-basket-case" kind of way, but I also didn't shy away from the issue at hand. Thankfully, she didn't get defensive, and we set about our own little plan to turn things around.

She started by buying herself a "food journal." In it, she wrote everything she ate on a daily basis and showed me so I could hold her accountable. This was a real eye-opener because, for the first time in a long time, she was really able to see what she was putting into her body. She complemented her eating habits by starting an exercise plan and taking daily vitamins.

It is now three years later, and Aly is definitely healthier. As a friend, it was important for me to look out for her and point out the blind spot she was oblivious to. But it was also vital for me to do it in a way that showed I loved her and simply wanted the best for her and her future.

At the end of the day, we need to remember the hard truth is sometimes the best truth. But in sharing the hard truth, we don't have to be hard while doing it. In fact, it would be wise of us to take note of an old Chinese Proverb: "Do not use a hatchet to remove a fly from your friend's forehead."

advice column

Q: I have become quite worried in the last few months about one of my best friends from school. She has been talking about how much she needs to lose weight, and lately I feel this has become an obsession for her. She eats only once a day and only eats veggies or salad. She is not overweight for her height but is determined to lose as much weight as possible before summer. Is this realistic? I have tried talking to her and telling her she is not fat or ugly, but it's like she can't understand the truth. Is there any way I can help her?

A: It sounds like your friend is suffering from a pretty low self-image, and she is determined to feel good about herself any way she can. In my experience, young women who are obsessed with dieting or losing immense amounts of weight in a relatively short period are actually compensating for other issues in their lives that they find difficult to deal with or find they cannot control, no matter how they try. These issues are usually about family breakdowns, rejection from others, feelings of suffocation or being controlled by another person, emotional stress, depression, physical or sexual abuse, or feelings of being abandoned by a parent or friend. These issues are the most common, but there could be all sorts of unaddressed issues going on for your friend, apart from her eating habits, that you may be unaware of.

Try talking to your friend about why she feels she needs to lose weight so dramatically. You may find it is her way of starting to feel good where she has felt really bad about herself for a long period of time. You may also be able to talk to her about other issues she is going through that have nothing to do with her body. Often eating disorders begin because a person cannot find any other outlet for self-expression.

You may also want to ask another person your friend trusts to talk to her about her preoccupation with her weight and why she is feeling so "fat." This friend may be a relative or trusted friend or someone a bit older who would know how to get her to open up about what is truly going on in her world.

This is not an issue you can tackle alone. I suggest you talk to your friend's mom or someone in her family, to alert them to what is happening or discuss with them the best approach to helping your friend. A counselor or health professional is someone I would strongly recommend if your friend doesn't respond to the concerns of those she knows. Eating disorders and control issues can be very deceptive to people who have them and often need professional intervention if they are allowed to progress too far. What is most important here is your friend's physical, emotional, and mental health, and I would take any appropriate steps to explain your concerns to your friend honestly and openly, and then refer her to someone who is qualified or experienced in this area and can really help her to go through a good recovery process.

Most importantly, continue to be a supportive friend and let her talk about her feelings. Your friendship and support will be most important to your friend as she starts to deal with some of the things that are happening in her life, her emotions, her relationships, and her body. Even if she seems hostile or angry at the beginning, she will truly appreciate you being there as she faces a possibly difficult or emotionally taxing time of admitting there is a problem, seeking help, and beginning her recovery. The key is that she knows she has your total support and the support of people she loves.

Lara's Story

I still remember the day my sister gave me the hard truth, and it hit me like a ton of bricks. I listened, reeling, angry, hurt, disbelieving, and feeling stubborn but knowing deep down inside it was only because she was right.

Just weeks earlier, I had been shopping with my boyfriend for a diamond ring; we were going ahead and making plans for our wedding and our future life together. We had told our parents, our pastors, and our close friends; everything was falling into place. Except that one little thought in the back of my mind that kept saying, "This should be the most exciting time of my life, my boyfriend should be thrilled that I've agreed to be his wife. After all, he is the one that asked me!" But he wasn't, and the closer we got to actually becoming engaged, the more distant he and I became.

I thought he just didn't want a fuss, but my sister, like others, saw differently. Sure, the wedding fit around his plans and what he wanted, and I was only too happy to oblige. Just as long as we were getting married, right? And then my sister said the words I didn't want to hear.

"Does he really want to get married? He says he loves you, he's committed, but is he willing to be selfless? Is he willing to think about your feelings, consider your needs? Or are you happy to go along with whatever he wants?"

I felt sick inside as the words sunk in. I was suspicious of the answer to those questions, but I was yet to confirm my doubts. Two days later, I drove to a café to meet my boyfriend for breakfast, knowing there was no turning back. I needed answers to those questions, as those nagging thoughts could no longer be ignored.

The conversation between my boyfriend and I that day became a blur. He gradually admitted he wanted to stick to his own plans, which left me with no choice but to say I wasn't prepared to be in a marriage where I wasn't a high priority.

We cried and walked away from each other, the shock still sinking in. It was an incredibly painful day, but most surprising was that I actually felt an incredible amount of peace. I knew at that point that my sister's honesty had meant my boyfriend and I could also be truthful with each other.

Since then, I still see this great guy around, and while it is sad that our relationship has ended, I'm so glad I had the courage to address something that could have caused me heartache in years to come.

I so often think that hearing the hard truth is a lot like removing a splinter—you might feel the pain of the splinter and know it's there, but you're kind of numb to it. However, if someone applies pressure to this spot, it can really hurt. You then have two choices: Either leave it there, where it will build up an infection and spread through your body, or face some more pain and dig it out, knowing that you will heal a lot better afterward. Believe me, the pain is worth it!

"Yes, we must ever be **friends**; and of all who offer you **friendship**, let me be ever the first, the **truest**, the **nearest** and **dearest**!"
HENRY WADSWORTH LONGFELLOW

by Amanda Spurling

girlfriendship

chapter 3: quiet torture
the silent treatment

"Friendship! Mysterious cement of the soul! Sweetener of life!"
ROBERT BLAIR

by Amanda Spurling

Quiet torture
the silent treatment

It was a cold, dark, and stormy night.

Well, actually I think it was a warm, balmy summer's night. But when I walked into the girls' bathroom in our church, my mood turned decidedly dark.

It was a normal Friday youth night, and standing at the sinks were two of our youth girls. One of them was inconsolable and being comforted by the other. I walked over to them and asked the one who was crying what was wrong. In between sobs, she told me that a group of girls was ignoring her. Earlier that night, when she walked up to her so-called friends to talk, they simply turned their backs and walked away, acting as though she didn't exist.

Suddenly the memories all came flooding back to me. No longer was I standing in the girls' bathroom of our church as a youth pastor; I found myself back in high school.

The biology lesson had just finished, and we were having our morning break. I knew something was wrong as soon as I walked up to my friend Roxanne, and she looked at me as though I didn't exist. I started to talk to her, but she coldly stared at me and walked away. I followed after her as she walked up to group of girls and started to chat with them happily. When I persisted in asking her what was wrong, she just kept ignoring me while her newfound friends started to laugh at me.

I walked away that morning hurt, angry, and confused, and to this day I still do not understand why girls inflict the silent treatment on one another. I've heard that the Chinese water torture inflicted on POWs is unbearable, but I think the silent treatment definitely comes in as a close second.

Girls know with precision how to "torture" other girls, and one of the most common methods of torture is when we ruthlessly and deliberately ignore one another. Some girls do it because it gives them a power rush. And I think that was the case with Roxanne. Looking back on our friendship, she liked to be the one in control. And giving me the silent treatment on a regular basis was her way of having power over my feelings.

In her hands she held a key of manipulation that locked me away in what seemed like solitary confinement. I felt lonely and alone. In some way, it gave her a rush to see how miserable she could make me, and it's no surprise that our friendship didn't last past the first year of high school.

Other girls give the silent treatment because they just feel like it. They wake up feeling moody and emotional, and being unable to articulate how they're feeling, they simply say nothing. And for those around them, it becomes a guessing game. We wonder what awful thing we've done to our friend to make her feel so moody and bend over backward to get her to say something, anything.

The silent treatment makes us feel like outcasts. It is unbearable because inside all of us is the need and desire to be noticed. When people notice us, we feel special, important, significant, and alive. That's why the silent treatment is so manipulative, because we'll do anything for our friends to pay attention to us, let alone talk to us.

Looking back now on that Friday night at youth group, I felt so angry that there were girls in our youth ministry who could be so cold toward their friend. It also made me feel incredibly sad because I knew how hurt this young girl was. In the end, I asked her if I could pray for her. I held her hand and asked God to comfort her and bring true friends into her life who would love and care for her.

There's an old saying that goes, "If you can't say something nice, don't say anything at all." But sometimes not saying anything does no good. And when we purposely say nothing out of spite, manipulation, or control, it erodes and eats away at our friendship until all that's left is an empty shell.

When it comes down to it, the choice is up to us what kind of girlfriendship we want. If we want our friendships to flourish and last, then we have to say something. We've got to resist keeping our mouths closed and allowing manipulation or control to rule our hearts.

True girlfriendship? The choice is ours.

by Amanda Spurling

"But **friendship** is **precious**, not only in the shade, but in the **sunshine** of life; and thanks to a benevolent arrangement of things, the **greater** part of **life** is sunshine."
THOMAS JEFFERSON

advice column

Q: My friend ignores me when she is angry with me. How can I make her realize that ignoring me is not the way to handle problems? She is acting very immaturely, and though I want to help her understand her behavior, I don't know what to say.

A: Here are some suggestions for dealing with the silent treatment from your girlfriends:

1. The next time your friend has a "silence episode," bring her attention to it. You will be amazed how many girls think it is perfectly natural for them to cease communication if they feel upset. Let your friend know that you need her to communicate her feelings to you rather than going silent.

2. Ask her why she is upset. Did you say something wrong? Did you do something wrong? What is causing her to react this way?

3. Be specific. Tell your friend exactly what you don't like about her reaction. How does it affect you? Do you feel ignored, mistreated, devalued? Perhaps as you explain your feelings, it will give your friend an idea of how to express her own feelings.

4. Let your friend know that you want her to find a different way of responding to her feelings and that you are willing to help her do this.

5. Let your friend know that you love her, that you want the best for her, and that you really want to work at communicating with her better, especially when she is upset. Knowing that you care enough to speak into her life about issues that concern you may be just what she needs to address her concerns confidently without shutting down emotionally or verbally.

Sarah's Story

*My immediate thoughts when I hear the word **friendship** are those girls in my life who've been through it all with me—the good times, bad times, sad times, disappointing times, celebration times—those people who have shared my life-changing moments.*

Over the past eleven years, there has been one particular friendship that has been so special to me. In this time, we've been best friends, worst enemies, and best friends again.

I met Nikki in 1992. I was just starting seventh grade, and Nikki had just moved to Perth from India. I distinctly remember the second day of school. I finally plucked up enough courage to go and speak to this girl who seemed so lost and alone. Back then I was a shy, soft-spoken girl who would rather walk the school yard alone than talk to a stranger, so for me I was taking a huge leap out of my comfort zone and placing myself in a position where I'd either be rejected or accepted. To this day I'm so glad I took the risk because this was the start of a great journey. Nikki and I would hang out both in class and during our breaks. Soon we became inseparable. As we got to know each other, we found out we had so much in common.

It was during this year that I was diagnosed with diabetes. While I was away from school, there was a lot of talk in my class about me, and a few people said I shouldn't return. This would be the first time I would find out who my friends were. Among all the gossip and rumors about me, Nikki stood up for me. She didn't really know what was going on with me, but she knew this—I was her friend and no one was going to talk about me.

Over the years, we have had our good and bad moments. We have had our petty fights, but we always seemed to work through our disagreements, which seemed to make our friendship stronger.

In 1997 we hit a point in our friendship when things just fell apart. One morning, I showed up at school only to be told by a mutual friend that Nikki no longer wanted to be my friend. More hurtful than this was the statement that Nikki never wanted to see me or talk to me ever again. For the rest of the week, I was in total shock. I was confused because Nikki seemed to hate me for no apparent reason. I was also heartbroken that she would ask a friend of mine to relay the message and angry that my friend agreed to it. I felt like my heart had been ripped out and thrown on the floor.

The days passed and turned into weeks, then months, and before I knew it, it was 1998. I was at a friend's 18th birthday party when Nikki walked in. It had been at least six months since I'd seen her, and I instantly wanted to be swallowed up by the ground. The last thing I wanted was a confrontation or to ruin my friend's party. To my surprise, Nikki came right up to me and started talking to me like nothing had happened. Apparently someone had taken my words, twisted them, and told Nikki that I'd said something I hadn't. From this incident, I learned the importance of going straight to my friends if I have a problem with something they've said or done, even though I don't like confrontation.

The night of the party, I drove Nikki home, and we had a good chat about things. I'm so happy that I didn't give up on ever being friends with her again. Since the party, we've had some amazing times together. I was the first person Nikki called when she got engaged, and I was bridesmaid at her wedding with the honor of helping her get dressed (and thus being the first person to see her in her wedding dress). I was also able to visit Nikki after the birth of her first and second child. We remain great friends and celebrated 10 years of friendship in 2002. Yes, we still have our disagreements, but I think it's fantastic that we can get along so well, even when we have different opinions.

I guess for me the main thing that I've learned through life is that to build a friendship that's worth having, you need to work on it. You have to put time and energy into it. You have to invest your heart into the friendship. Sometimes you even have to fight hard to save the friendship, but the rewards are priceless. What you have at the end is a friend you can rely on to be there for you through the good times and the bad.

girlfriendship

chapter 4: the ex factor
the phenomenon of "ex best friends"

"I count myself in nothing else so happy as in a soul rememb'ring my good friends."
WILLIAM SHAKESPEARE

The ex factor
the phenomenon of "ex best friends"

When I was a little girl, I lived on one of those neighborhood streets that little kids love to grow up on. Many a childhood fantasy was transformed into the real-life adventures of the Bank Street Gang, the name given to the miniature residents of our beloved street.

On one side of the street, modest homes sat nestled behind beautifully manicured lawns. On the opposite side, behind the bushes, a railway track spanned the entire length of our street. Visitors would wonder how we ever slept at night with trains whistling along at maximum speed. But most of us had been born into these homes. The mechanical rhythm of the trains going by had been our lullabies as infants, and like most things that become familiar over time, we barely noticed them after a while.

Perhaps the one part of this idyllic childhood that I consciously treasured was my friendship with Rachel B. I'm not sure what the "B" stood for. Five-year-olds are not always interested in details. Rachel and I had the kind of kindred bond that little girls are renowned for. We reveled in each other, we loved to be in each other's presence, and we were thrilled by our mutual hunger for adventure. Not to say that we didn't have our differences. She was the tomboy who climbed trees and loved lizards. I was the princess who wore glittery bracelets and refused to get my freshly polished nails dirty. But together we were formidable, a force to be reckoned with.

Rachel lived on Bank Street for three fun-filled years. But in the summer of the third year, Rachel's mom sat us both down and delivered the devastating news: Rachel's dad had found a new job and they were moving to another city.

It's funny how we remember some childhood moments our entire lives. The day Rachel left, I didn't get to say good-bye. I reached her house as the last moving truck drove off into the distance. I didn't know at eight years old what it meant to mourn, but I will never forget how I cried that day. My best friend in the universe was gone, and nothing could stop my heart from hurting.

Twenty years have passed since then. I no longer live on Bank Street, although I visit occasionally just to say hello to the trains as they whistle by. The memories of my childhood adventures come flooding back when I visit. In most of them, Rachel features prominently.

Other girls have graced my life since then, with their own brand of humor, adventure, and camaraderie. Some have stayed. These are the "lifers," the girls I treasure and couldn't imagine living life without. But others, like Rachel, have gone. Each one has left her mark, her signature brand of friendship that has truly enriched my life.

Sometimes, in my quieter moments, I wonder where they are, what they are doing, whether they are living their dreams and finding new adventures. Sometimes, I say a prayer that we will meet again one day. But each time I remember the happy times we shared, there is also a tinge of sadness.

Life gets so busy that we don't always pursue our friendships to the ends of the earth. Losing contact is not always inevitable. In some of my friendships, I have at times made the choice to lose touch, and it has cost me the richness of a lifetime shared.

You may have similar stories—friendships that have come and gone. Perhaps you too, in your quiet moments, remember those girls who brought life and laughter to your world. Maybe you too pray that one day you will have the most wonderful reunion. Maybe your friendship ended amidst hurt and betrayal. Maybe you grew apart for reasons you still don't quite understand. Whatever your story, my prayer for you is that you will cherish the girls you do have in your world today, that your value to each other will increase with time, and that each shared moment will be another chapter of the beautiful legacy of friendship you are building together.

Best friendships don't just happen. They take time and commitment. They take guts and hard work. They happen on purpose, not by chance. The phenomenon of "ex best friends" is common among girls, but one I believe we can change if we learn to be intentional and unconditional friends.

A famous proverb says, "One can put a thousand to flight, but two can put ten thousand to flight." Friendship is powerful, a formidable force on the planet. It's God's way of making life a rich experience. The opportunity to embrace and be embraced by a fellow pilgrim on the journey of life is the opportunity most girls dream of. Treasure it. Believe in its worth. Make it last a lifetime.

by Amanda Spurling

Never shall I **forget** the days I spent with you. Continue to be **my friend**, as you will always find me yours.

LUDWIG VAN BEETHOVEN

advice column

Q: My best friend and I had a huge falling-out just after our college graduation this summer. We were friends all through college, but we have not spoken for three months. She has since said things about me that are untrue and very hurtful. (She even told my boyfriend that I have an eating disorder, which is a huge lie.) I have tried to talk to her, but she refuses to return my phone calls. Her family and friends say she wants nothing to do with me. How can I make the situation better?

A: It sounds like your friend is still very hurt and angry. You say that you can't contact her by phone. Have you considered writing her a letter? Perhaps you could let her know that although you are both still obviously upset, you would like the opportunity to work things out. Perhaps you could ask her to verify the lies you have heard. Be specific. For example, "I have heard that you told my boyfriend I have an eating disorder. I would really like to know whether you remember saying anything like this to him. I am hopeful that we can talk in person and that we can sort out where things went wrong and how we recover from here."

Your friend will have one of two choices. The burden will be on her to get in contact with you once she receives the letter, allowing the two of you to get together and talk. Even if you decide to go your separate ways after this, you will have at least had the opportunity to clear the air. You may find that your friend is more than willing to work things out when she realizes you are trying your best to restore the relationship, not end it.

However, if your friend does not reply, you may need to cease contacting her. Even if it's for a few weeks or months, giving someone the space and time to calm down after a heated dispute or argument can be the best choice of action. It also stops the issue from escalating any further if at least one party is prepared to stop feuding.

If your friend never replies to your attempts to contact her, it may be her way of letting you know that she is not prepared to continue the relationship and that nothing you do will change her mind. In this case, you will need to accept that you have done your best to bring closure and resolution to the relationship and make a decision to move on with your life.

Amanda's Story

Today I got a text message from my mom informing me that my best friend from high school had just given birth to baby boy number four!

Wow. How different could two lives be?

If you had asked me twelve years ago who my best friend, closest companion, and partner in crime would be for life, I would have passionately declared Rebecca Ann! We both had many friends, the typical high school gaggle of girlfriends. However, Bec and my friendship was different. You could say we were inseparable. We had a deep connection that made us so much more than high school pals or university acquaintances.

On an emotional, spiritual, creative, and intellectual level, we just "got" each other. Our friendship deepened as we shared our deepest hurts, secrets, successes, and desires. It was within the safety of this friendship that I began to discover parts of my heart and life that I had hidden from my family and the world.

In retrospect, this relationship was pivotal to unlocking very deep parts of my soul. We traveled through a few heartbreaks, many long adventurous evenings, my parents' divorce, the devastating suicide of a close friend, an eating disorder, memorable holidays, and hilarious one-of-a-kind situations! We painted, talked, designed fashion, served, hung out, laughed, cooked, drank, smoked...generally lived out a typical teenage life together.

So what changed? Really simply, a guy came between us. I passionately fell in love with Him. You see, Bec liked this guy, too, but I fell completely head over heels for Him. I came to a place where I would do anything for Him, and Bec just didn't get me anymore. The guy I fell in love with was Jesus. The more I got to know Him, the more I realized that my life needed to change so I could live consistently.

This was when my friendship with Bec changed. No harsh words, no angry silences, no slammed doors, just a gradual realization that we were heading in very different directions. Two paths that had joined for a time were now splitting on the journey. I came to a place where the connection we once had became so different. It wasn't bad; I didn't judge her for the way she wanted to live her life. The season had subtly but irrevocably changed.

Bec got married (I was a bridesmaid), got pregnant, and bought a house. She is the beautiful mother of four boys, and truthfully, I have only seen two of them. I couldn't even tell you all their names. This is not something that I am proud of, and it makes me feel sad, but I know the decision to change the level of our friendship was a key one for me in the journey I was on.

Who knows? Bec and I may become closer friends again one day, but for now we have identical tattoos (a dare when we were seventeen), many beautiful memories, and lots of long stories to tell. She taught me to unlock some of the deep secrets that bound my emotions and soul. Then Jesus began to heal me from the devastating hurts that had been uncovered in our late-night chats. You could say that she prepared me for the love affair that I was to have. Now, her annual hug at someone's wedding, funeral, or birthday is a reminder of a poignant, life-defining friendship! Unforgettable.

girlfriendship

chapter 5: the ugly sister
gossip

"I cannot even imagine where I would be today were it not for that handful of friends who have given me a heart full of joy. Let's face it, friends make life a lot more fun."

CHARLES R. SWINDOLL

by Amanda Spurling

The ugly sister
gossip

A good friend of mine works in the same office as me. We have been friends since we were seventeen and eighteen, respectively. Our friendship has had its ups and downs, but we have always managed to get through the hard times and come out the other side smiling. One thing I love about our friendship is that we actually find it very easy to be honest with each other and to articulate how we are feeling.

The other day I was in her office, and as we were chatting, our conversation turned toward this chapter of the book. My friend was telling me about a few conversations she had had recently with different girls, conversations that had really amazed and disappointed her. In all of these conversations, young women she knew had confessed their hurt and frustration that others were talking about them behind their backs. These girls had been wounded by words that carried lasting impact and wielded great power, words of anger, words of untruth, words of strife, jealousy, and bitterness.

My friend's observations were not a surprise to me—they merely confirmed something Mary and I have recognized for years. So many conversations between girls and women can be liberating, uplifting, encouraging, and constructive. But many words we speak behind closed doors or in hushed whispers can wreak havoc on the girls we know (and even some we don't). It is very, very rare for a young man to get together with a group of young men in a restroom or coffee shop and begin to pick to pieces the lives, loves, and looks of other young men. The idea of this kind of all-guy gossip session is laughable. Why? Because most guys aren't prone to gossip, slander, or malice. These are a unique and unfathomable part of the female existence.

Let's face it, girls. Gossip and rumormongering are things we have all been part of. Even if we say nothing, it can be very tempting to listen to the latest "dirt" about who's grounded, who's dumped, who's drunk, who's mad, or who's wrong. Enthralling. Captivating. Harmless. Really?

What if it was you they were talking about? I once sat in a bathroom stall for half an hour as three girls who were supposed to be my friends talked about how much they disliked me. To this day, I still remember fighting back tears as I stood in that little space and listened to their "harmless" chatter. I could hardly breathe. My dress suddenly seemed too tight, and I felt like all the blood had drained from my heart. I was empty, numb, unable to believe how my "friends" could use such ugly, poisonous words to describe their contempt for me.

All of a sudden, I felt myself open the door wide and, to their absolute horror and embarrassment, calmly (or so they thought) walk to the sink, wash my hands, fix my hair, and walk out without giving them a sideways glance. No more than two minutes later, I was approached by one of the girls who assured me she didn't mean anything that she had said about me, and that she was only "pretending" not to like me so the other girls wouldn't be mad at her. She hoped we could still be friends and put this little "incident" behind us. Not likely.

That incident occurred when I was eighteen years old. I found out later that one of the girls was interested in some guy, and he had apparently rejected her advances and mentioned something about being interested in me. Needless to say, I had never spoken to this young man, much less become romantically involved with him. However, my very existence seemed to be a threat to these girls at that moment, and it made me the unsuspecting recipient of their wounding words.

One of the most amazing things about gossip is that it spreads so quickly. It's like a sore that starts as a tiny spot but over time gets more serious and becomes a raging rash, out of control and ready to demolish anything in its way. This is because we are very good at airing other people's laundry sometimes. Even if we don't consider ourselves gossipmongers (and no one ever does), we sometimes find it irresistible to be part of the "knowledge police"—to be one of those who measure and mark someone else's misfortune. When we give into this temptation, however, we are no better than those who deliberately spread lies and misinformation about others.

Talking about people behind their backs is anything but harmless. It causes those involved to become callous, to say things in secrecy that they would not have the courage to say to the victim. The undercurrent of gossip never fails to ruin friendships, reputations, relationships, or credibility. It leaves in its wake deep regret, punishment of innocents, suspicion, and question marks.

Gossipmongers reek of bravado, jealousy, and discontent. They too are victims in their own way—injured and insecure, lacking in wisdom and compassion, and happy to speak mercilessly about another individual just as long as the talk never turns on them. To be enlightened is one thing. But to contribute to the private or public humiliation of an innocent individual is another thing altogether.

Gossip is tantalizing. It can be deliciously seductive and altogether consuming. But it is never without intent. It is never innocent. It sears our consciences and causes us to think we are better than others and that somehow our words are justified. It causes us to accuse another's intentions, to malign another's character, to endanger another's reputation, and to judge another's motives. It's as ugly as it is alluring. It takes courage to defeat, and it will not make you popular if you refuse to participate. But it will make you dignified, and it will make you worthy of another's trust. And that, my friend, will give you every reason to smile.

"Ah, how **good** it feels...
the **hand** of an old
friend."
MARY ENGELBREIT

by Amanda Spurling

advice column

Q: This year I started attending a new school, and for the first couple of weeks, everything was great. I made new friends and hung out with a good group of girls who made me feel accepted. They even invited me to one of their sleepovers, which was really fun. But recently my new friends have been avoiding me. Whenever I'm around them, there is an uncomfortable silence, and I feel they don't want me as their friend anymore. This week I found out that a girl who also used to attend my previous school has been spreading rumors about me. She has been sending e-mails and telling people that I'm flirtatious, sleep around, and basically can't be trusted around guys. Now I have a reputation in my new school as being easy and loose, but it's all totally false. What can I do?

A: Unfortunately, gossip is a common communication weapon that is used to destroy and taint a person's reputation. It is usually done behind someone's back and is incredibly nasty, mean, and harmful. Even if the person who started the false rumor eventually apologizes by saying it was "all a big joke or misunderstanding," the damage has already been done. Whether the gossip is true, has shades of truth, or is completely false, some will still choose to believe it and others will just be confused and wonder what to believe. Meanwhile, those who know it to be false just hope that it will all go away—quickly.

I'm not sure why this girl has been gossiping about you, but often gossip is used as a form of conversation. Maybe she wanted to share something sensational or salacious to make her feel important or get some much-needed attention. Either way, you need to know how to handle the resulting fallout. So be calm, and be cool:

1. Be calm. Although you are probably fuming and very hurt, it's important not to cause a scene or confront the person who spread the lies about you in a public place. Speaking to her in an angry tone, having a public fit of tears, and accusing her will only make her feel vindicated in spreading her poison (and it is probably what she secretly wants). Wait until you have a clear head before facing her, and don't give her the satisfaction of seeing you break down. If you protest your innocence by freaking out and losing control, it only looks like you have something to hide. Also, don't be tempted to get back at this girl by starting your own gossip. Remember, you're better than that!

2. Be cool. Although you may be tempted to go around to each and every person in your school or call an assembly to tell them the truth, just be cool. When someone finally has the guts to tell you the rumors face-to-face, just say something like, "Wow, I wonder why someone would go to so much effort to spread a complete lie about me?" By displaying this type of attitude, it shows that you're not defensive, bitter, or resentful. It will also make others think that maybe the person who spread the gossip in the first place has a hidden agenda. In the end, people who have a habit of spreading lies and gossip will lose credibility and be viewed by others as untrustworthy. You, on the other hand, will be able to walk away knowing that you handled a messy and nasty situation with dignity and integrity, two qualities that will be lifesavers for you in the long run.

Therese's Story

Writing this story is quite a difficult task for me. There were so many rumors spread about me growing up that it is all just a blur. The rumors often started with a few people in my class, then they spread through my grade, and soon after throughout the school. Over the years, the kids who were my friends began to drift away until I was left on my own. They would smile and say hello from time to time, pretending that they liked me, but they would never sit with me or play with me during breaks.

I remember the day I arrived at school and there was a rumor going around that I was wearing pajama pants under my uniform. The girls circled me and questioned me about this until someone came up from behind me and pulled down my pants. This was humiliating and very embarrassing because even the boys were laughing.

As I entered high school, I became wary of people and never knew who to trust or talk to. The silly games and practical jokes had lessened, but the rumors continued. I remember being aware of how I felt: sad and alone. Sad because it hurt when I heard what they were saying and alone because nobody could understand how horrible the experience was. For fear of rejection, I shut the world out.

Then after I graduated from college and relocated, I moved in with four other girls who would teach me what friendship was. We lived across the road from a house of guys, and looking back, it was like a TV sitcom. During this time I learned about trust, loyalty, and companionship. I learned that I am worthwhile and that my feelings matter and my opinion counts. I learned to enjoy life and have fun by playing practical jokes on the boys as they continued to outdo us. I began to believe that I am a good person and I am likeable. I had developed a sense of belonging and, through it, a hope for my future.

More recently, my new roommate had a friend visit her, and when we were introduced, she claimed to have gone to school with me. In that instant I feared that my world was *about to fall apart. The rumors had returned to haunt me, and maybe I didn't deserve this new life I was living. As the week went by, I anxiously waited...and then nothing... no rumors, no bad stuff, and I realized that things were perhaps different now.*

What happened? I stopped believing the lies. I stopped seeing myself how others saw me, and over time my identity was no longer in the rumors. I went to church and met some new friends who believed in me and encouraged me. Through this I have learned to value friendship. When you find a friend you can confide in because she is loyal, honest, and supportive, one who is nonjudgmental through your ups and downs and accepting of all your faults, then you have a good friend.

Second, through knowing who Christ is, I began to know who I am, and with the security of knowing this, I found freedom in forgiveness. When you let go of the rumors and the lies and the people who have done you wrong, you are set free from the pain and sadness that it brought you. I don't know how or why, but I know that forgiveness is the key.

girlfriendship

chapter 6: let's celebrate
enjoying each other's victories

"Where there are friends, there is wealth."
TITUS MUCCIUS PLAUTUS

Let's celebrate
enjoying each other's victories

Have you ever seen the movie *I Am Sam*? It's a story of remarkable courage and unconditional love against all the odds. Sam is a mentally challenged man with the intellect of a seven-year-old and the heart of a hero. He is in love with life and completely and selflessly loves Lucy, his seven-year-old daughter, whom he has raised alone from birth.

There is a scene in that movie that I have never forgotten. Lucy is reading a book with her dad before bed, a practice the pair has enjoyed since Lucy was very young. However, this new book has some big words that Sam is having trouble pronouncing. Lucy recognizes this very quickly, and not wanting to outdo her dad, she also pretends to be perplexed by these words. Sam knows his daughter is pretending and demands that she read the words. Lucy flatly refuses. When Sam questions why Lucy doesn't want to read, she explains softly, "I don't want to read the word if you can't." Sam replies, "Don't you see? I want you to read the word. It makes me happy when you read."

In this short exchange, Sam is a true teacher. He teaches his little girl that the sign of a true friend is someone who delights in another's success. Although he cannot read at the same level as Lucy, he is enthralled by her progress and wants to celebrate her achievement, even though he knows he will never keep up with her.

I love this dialogue between this loving daddy and his daughter. I love that this man is not concerned with his own limitations or pride but has such a pure desire for his daughter to move into new dimensions of development. Human greatness exists not in intellectual profundity but in our ability to celebrate and share in the successes and triumphs of another.

Mary and I have been best friends for six years. In all those years, she has proven her friendship, her loyalty, and her love in so many ways. But one thing that has been such a joy to me is her ability to share uninhibitedly in my greatest moments without a hint of jealousy, insecurity, or despondency. She has truly reveled in my success, and she has shared in my most cherished moments. I love her for that.

I love how she has made my victories her reason to dance, to sing, to celebrate. I love how she made my bridal shower the most beautiful, glamorous affair I could have dreamed of. (She later won a national magazine prize for her efforts!) I love how she worked tirelessly on my wedding day to get me to the church almost on time! And how she still managed to look utterly amazing as she walked down the aisle ahead of me. I love how hers was one of the first faces I saw hours after the birth of my baby girl. I love the teddy bear she wrapped with such care that is now my daughter's favorite toy. We take it with us everywhere we go. I cherish the beautiful christening outfit that Mary so generously gave my little girl even though, by family tradition, it was meant to be worn by her own firstborn daughter, an event we still eagerly await!

We have chosen to be friends who delight in each other's successes. Each of us has applauded loudly and vigorously as life has smiled at the other. My wedding day, the publication of her first book, the arrival of our children, awards and accolades, so many precious and prized moments—all have been made even richer by the fact we each had the other to help celebrate the moment. These are memories I will never forget, memories I will cherish throughout my lifetime and into eternity.

I'm sure we'll go trekking through heaven together. And as we set up camp on the banks of paradise, we will look back on a lifetime of joint celebrations and multiplied joys—victories made even sweeter in their sharing.

Thus nature has no **love** for solitude, and always leans, as it were, on some **support**; and the **sweetest** support is found in the most **intimate friendship**.

really difficult. My friend is beautiful, smart, and really popular. She always seems to get everything she wants, and to be really honest, sometimes I resent her for it. I don't want to be envious of my friend, but I can't help feeling a little bit left out in the cold. What should I do?

It's pretty common for girls to feel inferior in the presence of other girls at times. There is always going be someone to compare ourselves to—someone more attractive, more intelligent, more athletic, more artistic, more spiritual, or more sophisticated can seem to hijack the attention of others just when we have made a conscious effort to look or do our best. However, this is sometimes more a statement about our own insecurities than another girl's desire to steal the limelight.

My suggestion is twofold. Let your friend know how you feel. This will take some courage, but at least your friend may try to be more sensitive toward you. She may also reassure you of your great qualities or even help you take inventory of what you would like or need to change. Maybe your friend feels that you have qualities she admires, and maybe she also feels slightly envious of your great fashion sense or incredible character qualities like loyalty, compassion, or trustworthiness.

Here's an exercise I often give to young women who are battling issues of unhealthy self-esteem:

1. Write a list of all the things you absolutely love about yourself. For example, you may love your sense of humor or the color of your eyes.

2. Write a list of all the things you like about yourself—things that may not be significant or noticeable to others, but YOU know they make you feel good about yourself. This list may include things like a patient nature, a talent for cooking, an ability to listen to those in crisis, or slim, strong ankles. Anything at all that you feel good about.

3. Lastly, make a list of all the things you would change about yourself if possible. This list may include what you would change about your looks, your fashion sense, your character, or what you wish you could do better. Some of these things will be "fixable," and others won't. This list may include things like being a better communicator, knowing what to say when a gorgeous guy makes eye contact with you, getting braces for your teeth, playing the flute better, learning to paint, or playing tennis better.

Take a good look at all three lists. Are they even? Or do you have a list of wishes and wants that far outweighs your list of what you like and love about yourself? If this is the case, chances are that your self-esteem has taken a bit of a battering and your insecurities about your friend's achievements are really a not-so-subtle indicator of your own feelings of unworthiness or unattractiveness. Envy and jealousy can reveal a lot about our self-worth. It's important that you are not defeated by the accolades another individual receives and that you don't use these as a measure of your own success.

The best friends are the ones who share each other's victories and are confident in their own abilities. As you begin to see yourself as a worthy candidate for accolade and affection, you will see your friend as less of a threat to your happiness and security.

Heather Jayne's Story

Growing up I was always seen as the girl who had a lot of male friends. But truthfully, I have always had amazing female friends—best friends who are teaching me what true friendship is all about, friendship that you can only find with girls...

Like the best friend with whom I shared overwhelming emotions and memories of the amazing Australian outback when her family invited me to travel up the coast with them. Knowing that I was able to share experiences of Aboriginal culture, scary alligators, and muddy farmland that we can always look back on.

The best friend who was there with comforting arms and encouraging words the moment she found out my dad had passed away, sending me flowers and almost getting fired from work when she walked out because she wasn't going to let me do the funeral on my own. Knowing that I didn't have to do it alone and having someone there to pick up the pieces and keep me strong.

The best friend who can just sit and eat sweets with me when I am fed up with the boy I've just argued with, or when people just get to be too much, no matter how many calories are involved. Making things all okay by having fun and joking around with me. Knowing that I can let go of all of life's glitches and stresses through the simple act of side-splitting laughter.

The best friend who listens to my dreams and aspirations, and when it all seems too hard, pushes me on. Who challenges me to dream big dreams and then accomplish them. Even when she has the hassles of maintaining a house and raising kids, she allows me a chance to express how I feel but not a chance to whine and complain. Knowing that she has faith that I will accomplish all I dream while, at the same time, not letting me carry on about silly, pointless things.

The best friend who hugs me for no reason and tells me that I'm strong and beautiful. Making sure that I know I am a princess who can fight good fights and finish the race like a champion even when I don't feel like I am one.

The best friend I have grown up with and who knows me inside out. Being able to share our deepest secrets (like sneaking out of the house together and putting bubble bath in the school fountain). Knowing that no matter how bad the punishment, she would never reveal any of it to anyone and that even with all that information, she still loves me.

The amazing thing is that each of these is a different friend. I thank God that I have so many wonderful girlfriends to share my life with. There is one thing I keep coming back to that I think is the key to really good friendships. It's not actually what my friends say or do that is important, but it is having the knowledge that the love, comfort, support, and encouragement is there for me even before I ask for it, and no matter what the experience. This knowledge is what gives me wings when I've forgotten how to fly.

girlfriendship

chapter 7: guycentric
when he means more than she does

"I thank You, God in heaven, for friends."
MARGARET SANGSTER

SURF RE

by Amanda Spurling

Guycentric
when he means more than she does

My husband and I first met in our eighteenth year of life. For me, it was definitely love at first sight, although I stubbornly refused to admit it! Marcus was the complete embodiment of every strong, handsome knight I had ever conjured up in my imagination. With his dark hair, smooth olive skin, captivating mystery, smoldering dark eyes, and a smile to die for, I thought he was the most incredible specimen of the male species I had ever laid eyes on.

Our first interaction was a moment I will never forget. We were both at a youth leadership camp. I had just been for a swim and was walking back through the main house when I saw him lying on a bed, nursing his bandaged foot. I thought he looked gorgeous in his two-dollar track pants and white T-shirt. I still remember how my tummy turned somersaults as I casually sauntered past him, pretending not to notice his existence.

Later that night, we had our first actual conversation. I was in the meeting room with a couple of girlfriends when he limped into the room and took a seat nearby. As our eyes connected, he leaned toward me. His breath was warm, with strong overtones of peppermint-flavored gum as he asked sweetly, "Are you using that cushion?" "No," I replied. Marcus took the cushion and placed it under his foot. That was it. The most romantic moment of my life to that point!

Trust me, I know what you're thinking. In the retelling, it does sound pretty uneventful. Certainly it was not the way I imagined I would meet my future husband. The story of our first meeting is hardly a tale that will have our future grandchildren sitting on the edge of their seats as we tell it! But it's our story, and I get goose bumps whenever I reminisce about that first encounter.

To say that our relationship went from strength to strength after that would be an utter and complete lie. Our relationship was a supreme drama of the on-again, off-again variety. It took eight years for us to walk down the aisle and enter the world of wedded bliss we enjoy today.

In my late teens and early twenties, I really struggled with the idea that a guy like Marcus could actually love me—warts and all. I lived in constant fear that he would be whisked off by another, more beautiful, more sophisticated, less neurotic girl, and I would be left pondering yet another failed romance!

The reason for my great insecurity was largely paranoia. I know that now. But at the time, I certainly had convincing evidence that there were some evil stepsisters in our tale who would gladly steal my prince. These fears were cemented one night at a birthday party we organized for Marcus. We had invited a friend of his. Annabelle was beautiful, blond, intelligent, and very intimidating. However, she and I had begun to develop a really great friendship. We had all gone out together quite a few times, and although she didn't have a boyfriend, she was always telling me how lucky I was, how wonderful Marcus was, and how she would love to be with a guy like him. I should have read these warning signs, but I really trusted Annabelle, especially since she and Marcus had known each other for years.

However, that night, I noticed that Annabelle was acting quite distant and funny toward me. Her words were sharp and sarcastic. This was a side of her I had not noticed before. I couldn't help but wonder what I had done wrong. Throughout the night, she seemed to steer the conversation toward funny incidents, nostalgic moments, and unforgettable events that predated my relationship with Marcus. This made me feel very out of the picture. Although Marcus tried to include me in the conversation, most of what this young lady spoke about was completely foreign to me. Needless to say, I began to feel rather uncomfortable.

The crescendo came later on that night. Annabelle was very eager to show Marcus the present she had bought for him. Before my eyes, she took a bottle out of a beautifully packaged box and gave it to him. A beautifully handwritten note accompanied the bottle. I couldn't see what it said but thought to myself what a nice present it looked like. When Marcus opened the present, he managed a brisk "thank you" and stuffed the bottle back in its box.

The next day, Marcus showed me the gift from Annabelle. In bright, large letters, the words "MASSAGE OIL FOR BODY" were neatly printed on the bottle. The pretty note that accompanied the present read, "If you ever need a massage, just let me know." I was absolutely horrified—and very mad. This girl was supposed to be a friend to both of us.

The saddest part of this melodrama was that this was not the only time that Annabelle had treated a close friend this way. We later heard that she had made a move on her best friend's boyfriend. Unfortunately, her attempt was successful, but the relationship was short-lived.

I found it hard to imagine why a girl as beautiful and popular as Annabelle would need to be so devious and why she had acted in such a bizarre way. Marcus couldn't believe that she was so different from the girl he had known for so many years. Annabelle had never shown any interest in Marcus in a romantic way before this, and he was saddened by her actions. In the end, it had a great impact on their friendship, and she soon moved on without us.

Ten years later, my job as a youth pastor means I spend much of my time counseling teen and twenty-something girls. It amazes me how many similar stories I see and hear of beautiful, successful girls who are not able to resist the attraction of another girl's guy. I talk with so many heartbroken girls who suffer at the hands of these rather intimidating but insecure "other women." Though they feel sorry and sad for these girls, it is still hard for them to believe that girls they know and love would try to "steal" their men.

I have seen and experienced enough of this ugly side of girlfriendship to last a lifetime. I have seen girls who grow into women consumed with envy at the joy of a friend in love. These are sad, unhappy, and restless women. They are what I term "guycentric" girls. Woman who, regardless of age or achievement, have one common bond—they crave the attention of a significant male in the life of a girl they know, and they feel compelled to compete for his attention. Each has her own reason for this compulsion—jealousy, insecurity, rejection, even psychological or emotional imbalance.

I have also seen enough women recover from this disease of insecurity to be heartened that "guycentricity" is not terminal. I know many young ladies who have beaten this threat to their happiness and have become secure, emotionally mature, relationally aware women, wives, and friends.

There are so many beautiful, amazing treasures that come with girlfriendship. We are women. We are allies. We are sisters. Let's never fail to honor the dignity and God-intended design of girlfriendship. Let's build bonds that are unbreakable, no matter how great the temptations are that come. Let's live out beautiful friendships that are marked with the indelible ink of loyalty.

We owe it to ourselves.

"It's the little things that matter, that add up in the end, with the priceless thrilling magic found only in a friend."
ELIZABETH DUNPHY

by Amanda Spurling

advice column

FLIRTING is one of those incredibly deceptive behaviors that seem so innocent and fun at the time but can lead to some serious repercussions.

Following are three myths about FLIRTING that every girl needs to know:

Myth No 1.
FLIRTING is an innocent, accidental behavior.

Whether they admit it or not, everyone knows when they are flirting and why. FLIRTING helps us attract male attention when we need it most—when we feel insecure about how we look or how popular we are or how valuable we are as women. FLIRTING is not just about how you approach a member of the opposite sex; it is also about how you dress, how you speak, and how you think about guys. FLIRTING can not only cause other girls to feel threatened by you but can also cause members of both sexes not to take you seriously, no matter how intelligent you are. FLIRTING has less to do with attraction and everything to do with asserting influence or power over another person.

Myth No 2.
FLIRTING is something you can easily switch off when you get married or enter into a long-term relationship.

FLIRTING is like any other practiced habit: The longer you have been doing it, the longer it takes to recover from it or change course. When you enter into a long-term relationship, you take into that relationship everything about you, everything within you. The problem occurs when you haven't dealt with issues that can hinder that relationship while you were single. A good friend of mine has been married for three years. Before she was married, she struggled with the issue of FLIRTING for years. She once said that she would have qualified for a PhD in FLIRTING! When she got married, she made a vow to her husband that she would tell him of any time she felt inclined to FLIRT with another man. Throughout the years, she has kept that vow, knowing that her marriage does not negate the temptation to seek affirmation or attention from members of the opposite sex to reinforce her own value.

Myth No 3.

FLIRTNG is just a natural part of some people's personalities.

No, it's not. Even the most extroverted, fun-loving, uninhibited person knows when they are overstepping the FLIRTATION mark. It's important to realize that FLIRTING is not a subconscious, natural habit like breathing or walking. FLIRTING isn't an inherent part of anyone's personality. It is something we learn, something we practice and cultivate, and something that we can master. It doesn't matter if you are loud, quiet, a talker or a non-talker, blond or brunette, blue-eyed or brown-eyed, right-handed or left-handed. FLIRTING is not something that is natural; it is a cultivated power maneuver as potent as strong perfume and as punchy as a kickboxing class.

As women, we need to be aware of our treatment of the opposite sex and how our relationships with guys can affect our relationships with girls. Wise up: Your flirting can lead to awful consequences, including broken hearts and devastated friendships.

Tina's Story

My best friend's name is Leanne. We met in first grade and hit it off right away. Never could we have imagined at such a young age the lifelong friendship we had begun to build. We were best friends all the way through elementary school, and we spent all our time together.

Eighth grade was a pretty hard year for us. There was big intake of girls into our school. Leanne is a very charismatic person, and everyone wants to spend time with her. I found myself feeling pretty protective over her at this time, and I didn't really like the idea of others getting too close to her. I was really insecure, and the thought of losing Leanne's friendship was a little frightening. There were two particular girls that openly wanted to tear Leanne and my friendship apart. The only way they knew how to get close to Leanne was to come between us and try and turn Leanne against me. On the outside, I just acted like I didn't care and hung out with my other friends, but on the inside, I was hurting pretty bad.

In ninth grade, things started to settle. I realized that I had to become more secure in myself (which is a lot easier said than done) and that the other girls could say whatever they wanted to tear me down, but Leanne and I would always be the best of friends. I had to constantly remind myself that I didn't have to compete with them for her friendship. I started to spend more time with Leanne and the other girls that had been causing problems for me. It ended up that they weren't all that bad. In this same year, one of our very close friends died from an overdose, and it was a pretty rough time. I don't think we could have dealt with it as well as we did if we hadn't had each other's support through that time.

Guys have been a bit of a downfall for us a couple of times. We haven't let guys get in the way of our friendship; we just have different standards and beliefs when it comes to certain things. For example, Leanne was with one of my exes a few times. Because I didn't have such a serious relationship with the guy, she figured that meant it was okay for her to be with him, whereas in my books, best friends just don't go out with each other's exes. Period. Another time was earlier this year when we were going out with two guys who were best friends. I was with Joel, Leanne was with Zac. After I broke up with Joel, Leanne told me that Joel had been with another girl while we were going out. She hadn't told me earlier because she was told not to, but she figured it was okay now since I'd broken up with Joel. This made me question where her loyalties lay.

After all the drama with trust issues, guys, and other things, little frustrations began to build up. I started feeling really bitter toward her and just didn't want to be around her. At the same time, I really missed her, and she didn't know what was up with me, so I figured if I couldn't face talking to her, I'd write her a letter. By getting everything out in the open first, we were able to just work our way through it all. There have been a few times in our friendship when we just needed to take time out from each other. But we both know that no matter how long we haven't talked, or how big a fight we have had, we will always sort it out after we've taken the time to cool off and think straight. Sometimes it's taken a few days, other times a few weeks.

It is so hard to put thirteen years of friendship into a short little summary. This has focused on some of the messy times in our friendship; however, there have been so many more great times than bad. We've got great trust between us now and know that we can say pretty much anything and not be judged for it. We spend tons of time hanging out and talking, and if something's up, we both know that we just need to make the call and we'll be there for each other. We've got so many great memories from the last thirteen years, and it's always fun to remember the "good old days"; it helps us appreciate the great friendship we have. We've shared so many laughs and tears, good times and bad. Our friendship has been tested in so many ways, but it's only made it that much more rewarding. We complement each other in a great way and are always learning from each other. Spending time together is always a blast. I absolutely love her to bits. Life wouldn't be the same without her.

girlfriendship

We will be friends until forever, just you wait and see. We will be friends until forever,

chapter 8: who you gonna call?
dependability

"We will be friends until forever, just you wait and see."
WINNIE THE POOH

by Amanda Spurling

Who you gonna call?
dependability

Don't you just hate getting woken up when you're having one of those once-in-a-lifetime dreams—dreams about winning a million dollars (no, make that a billion dollars), flying carefree through the air, discovering you're a multi-talented diva, or winning that prized golden Oscar?

I can't remember exactly what I was dreaming about when I was woken up at 3:00 a.m. by the phone ringing, but I know it must have been a goody because I do remember being very annoyed, cranky, and thinking to myself, "How rude. I haven't even given my acceptance speech yet!"

I stumbled about of bed, fuzzy-haired and blurry-eyed. My husband had answered the phone before me, and I could tell something was wrong. On the other end was Aly, calling from Chicago (she had gone over to do a youth internship). My husband handed the phone to me, and in between the periods of sobs and silences, I was able to decipher that Aly was desperately homesick. She missed her friends, family, and everything that was familiar to her. Over the next hour or so, we talked and talked and (as only girls can do) talked. By the end of the phone call, she was feeling better and determined to finish her U.S. internship. I simply went back to bed and tried to redream my pre-phone dream.

Looking back on that phone call, I have to say that there is something special about having a friend that you can call any time of the day or night. In fact, Marlene Dietrich said it best: "It's the friends you can call up at 4:00 a.m. that matter."

Girlfriendship is about having that special friend who you can share the darkest times and the best of times with. And there are two types of friendships you can have: a text message friendship or a voice recognition friendship.

An text message friendship is where we play it safe. We never venture out too far, conversationally speaking. We banter about superficial things like the "SXY GUY," our "GR8 W'END," and occasionally ask meaningful questions like "R U OK?" Text message friendships are quick, easy and cheap but not "NTIRLY S@ISFY'G."

On the other hand, a voice recognition friendship is exactly that. We instantly recognize the voice on the other end of the line and don't even have to ask who is calling because they're so familiar to us. It's the friend we call when we get that dream job or when our dreams have been dashed. It's the type of friendship that requires time, effort, expense, and risk in opening ourselves up, but it is also unbelievably nourishing to our souls.

Life deserves more than just shallow friendships and amiable acquaintances. We need other girls in our lives who "recognize" our voices and who connect with us in a deep way. This is what true girlfriendship is, and I am incredibly blessed to have a friend who recognizes my voice—Aly. Without a doubt, she is the friend I could call for emergencies, celebrations, PMS days, or quick chats. Not surprisingly, she is also the friend who I have the most unforgettable memories with, both good and bad. Unlike text mesages that can be easily deleted and forgotten, it's a lot harder to erase conversations that are etched on your soul. But I wouldn't have it any other way.

Although we go through times in our lives where we sometimes wonder if we'll ever make it out the other side, there's something incredibly reassuring in knowing that we have friends we can count on and who know us deeply. The Bible says, "A friend loves at all times," and one of the best things about girlfriendship is having friends we can depend on at all times...even at 3:00 a.m.

advice column

Q: My girlfriends and I have always been there for each other. We have a great relationship, but lately one of our friends has been getting into all kinds of trouble and we don't know what to do with her. She has been accused of shoplifting, has racked up huge phone bills that she is unable to pay, and is currently seeing a guy who she knows is dating another girl. She has confided in us and is really honest about where her life is at but doesn't seem to change, despite her promises. We are all really worried about her, but she keeps telling us not to overreact! Please help us. She has become very erratic and impulsive. How can we get through to her?

A: Your friend is very fortunate that she has such caring girlfriends who want to help her and be there for her. However, even if we have the most admirable of intentions, we cannot live our friends' lives for them. The number one issue here is whether your friend really feels she wants and needs to change her lifestyle. If she does, her desire to change will be reflected in the decisions she makes. Is your friend just saying what you want to hear, or are you seeing her make life-altering decisions and changing her behavior? No matter how much you want things to be better for your friend, she is the only one who can make the necessary changes that would get her life on track.

You may need to sit down and have a good heart-to-heart chat with your friend and let her know how worried you are about her current activities. You have indicated that although your friend makes promises, there is not a lot of convincing evidence of her desire to deal with these dramas in her life. Your friend needs to make a number of moral, ethical, and relational decisions before any change will come. If you talk till there is no breath left in your lungs, and she is still unconvinced of her need to change, or unprepared to make right choices, your words are unfortunately not going to be enough. People can learn the easy way or they can pay heavy consequences for undisciplined ways of living. I pray your friend endeavors to arrest her situation and begins to choose right. Your prayers and concerns for her are only part of the solution—she must make the next move. Thankfully, she has great support to do so.

"All our **young** lives we search for someone to **love**, someone who makes us **complete**. We choose partners and change partners. We dance to a song of heartbreak and **hope**, all the while wondering if somewhere and somehow there's someone searching for us."

THE WONDER YEARS

Karlee's Story

It was at the beginning of eleventh grade that I met Shannon. She came to my school from another school and we instantly "clicked." We became best friends, and we did absolutely everything together. Every weekend we would stay at each other's house, and at school we would always be together. In fact, if people saw us apart they would ask us, "Where's your other half?" We were practically joined at the hip. We knew everything about each other and could talk to each other about anything. We had the best friendship. That is, until we got boyfriends.

We had both liked these guys and thought it would be fun if we had boyfriends at the same time. The first few months were fine; everything seemed to be cool and simple. Then I broke up with my boyfriend while Shannon and her boyfriend started to get more serious about their relationship and spend a lot more time together.

By this time we were in twelfth grade. I became very jealous and felt like I was no longer the most important person in Shannon's world. We would still sit together, but her boyfriend would always be with us, and I would feel very uncomfortable when they got kissy and cuddly in front of me. Besides, we couldn't talk about the same stuff when he was around.

Looking back now, I can see that I had a lot of insecurities and that what I did was wrong. I stopped talking to Shannon as much and acted upset with her for no reason. I did this because I wanted her to see that I was unhappy with our new arrangement, and I didn't want to confront her about it. I wanted her attention and didn't know how else to get it. Of course, I didn't want to admit that I was jealous, so I tried to make it seem that everything was Shannon's fault. Unfortunately, I let this carry on for quite a while, instead of being straight up, sorting out the issues, and telling her how I truly felt.

Consequently, we gradually grew apart until we hardly even talked anymore. This hurt both of us so much. I wrote her a few letters later just to apologize for the stupid way I had acted and let her know how sorry I was. We tried to get our friendship back to the way it had been, but it was never the same again. I know now that if I had sorted out my issues earlier, none of this would have happened. Shannon didn't really do anything wrong, and I really regret the way I acted toward her.

It's been a couple of years since then, and we are still friends, but we hardly see each other now. Shannon is still with her boyfriend. They are both wonderful people, and I am very happy for them. Even though things didn't turn out that well, I am so thankful for the good times we did share. I learned so much from our friendship.

Since then, God has blessed me with some incredible friends, and I am able to take what I have learned and apply it to these friendships. I have also been able to deal with the issues I had developed in my friendship with Shannon. I have realized that friendships, especially friendships with other girls, are so important. I have learned to treasure these friendships and work at them no matter what. I have learned to be open and honest and to admit when I am wrong.

Friendships are made to be treasured. Don't let them slip away. Good friends truly are a gift from God.

others, and about how others make room for us. Friends

at the end of the day, about the way we make room for oth

d about how others make room for us. Friendship is, at

d of the day, about the way we make room for others, a

out how others make room for us. Friendship is, at the e

the day, about the way we make room for others, and ab

w others make room for us. Friendship is, at the end of

y, about the way we make room for others, and about h

hers make room for us. Friendship is, at the end of the c

out the way we make room for others, and about how oth

ake room for us. Friendship is, at the end of the day, about

y we make room for others, and about how others make ro

us. Friendship is, at the end of the day, about the way

ake room for others, and about how others make room for

iendship is, at the end of the day, about the way we make ro

others, and about how others make room for us. Friends

at the end of the day, about the way we make room for oth

d about how others make room for us. Friendship is, at

d of the day, about the way we make room for others, a

out how others make room for us. Friendship is, at the end

e day, about the way we make room for others, and about h

hers make room for us. Friendship is, at the end of the c

out the way we make room for others, and about how oth

ake room for us. Friendship is, at the end of the day, ab

e way we make room for others, and about how others ma

om for us. Friendship is, at the end of the day, about the w

e make room for others, and about how others make room

girlfriendship

chapter 9: all about me
one-sided friendships

"Friendship is, at the end of the day, about the way we make room for others, and about how others make room for us."
BETH KEPHART

by Amanda Spurling

All about me
one-sided friendships

One of my earliest memories is of going to kindergarten in a small town called Nhulunbuy in Northern Australia.

I was four years old, and I absolutely loved the tricycles. Every day I looked forward to scooting around the "rally track" on my "treddly deddly." But as fate would have it, all the other kindergarteners loved the trikes, too, and many times I missed out on a ride because someone else had beaten me to them.

One day, I decided no one was going to beat me to the trikes, but first I had a challenge to overcome. The kindergarten had a rule that all the kids had to eat their morning snack before they were allowed to play outside. So on this particular morning, I was determined to stuff that food down my throat as fast as possible and then make a speedy dash for my speed machine.

So as quick as I could, I shoved my banana into my mouth, and with my cheeks bulging (and in between chewing and swallowing), I made a dash for the trikes and hopped on the red one. With adrenelin pumping through me and feeling totally exhilarated, I furiously peddled around the track like a kid possessed. However, after a couple of record-breaking laps, I started to feel sick. Halfway through my third lap my tummy started to do an alien on me and suddenly, without warning, I threw up chunky banana all over the trike and the track. Not surprisingly, no one wanted to go near me or the trikes for the rest of the day!

That day I learned an important life-changing lesson: "No one likes a banana-hurling rev-head."

But there were other important lessons I learned in kindergarten.

I learned to share to wash my hands after going to the bathroom, to be polite, to cooperate, and not to pick my nose while in the middle of finger painting. Kindergarten is where many of life's social skills are learned and where we start to form fun, carefree friendships.

Basically, a friend in kindergarten is the one who holds your hand when you've got to get into pairs, shares the LEGOS® with you and gives you the bright pink crayon when only that and the dull gray one are left. And when it comes down to it, that's really the best description of a friend...someone who looks out for you rather than just herself.

James F. Byrnes said, "Friendship without self-interest is one of the rare and beautiful things in life." Unfortunately, friendship dominated by self-interest seems more the norm and is commonly known as one-sided friendship, or the Me, Myself, and I Malady. A good way to figure out whether you are in a one-sided friendship is to look honestly at your friendships and ask yourself some questions:

• When your friend calls you, does she always seem to talk about herself?
It's only human nature that we want to talk about ourselves and tell others about all that's happening in our corner of the universe. But when all you hear about are the events that shape your friend's world and you can't get a word in edgeways, sideways, or any which way, then it's not an equal friendship.

• Does it mysteriously seem that every topic of conversation is twisted back to your friend?
Don't you just hate it when you tell your friend something exciting and she butts in and says those annoying words, "That's exactly what happened to me too, blah, blah, blah"? She just seems to have a gift of headlining everything back to herself, and in the process makes your story yesterday's news.

• Do you ever feel used and taken for granted?
Friendship is about give-and-take. But do you feel that your friend only calls you to ask for something, borrow something, or when she needs you for something? If this is the case, it can make you feel frustrated, annoyed, and angry, especially when you simply call her to say hi.

A good friend is someone who gives equal amounts into the friendship as you do. However, there will be times and seasons where the balance of giving in the friendship will weigh more on one particular person, and that's okay.

It's also important to be aware that sometimes the longer the friendship, the easier it is to take each other for granted, mainly because we think our friend will always be there for us. But that is not necessarily the case. Long friendships are always at risk of ending when either of the friends involved doesn't feel respected or valued.

At the end of the day, girlfriendships really do take effort and (to be honest) sometimes we simply can't be bothered with the whole give-and-take thing. But believe me, the world would be a very uninteresting and bland place if was just all about you or me.

So in the wise words of Robert Fulghum, "No matter how old you are, when you go out into the world, it is best to hold hands and stick together."

"We cannot tell the precise moment when friendship is formed. As in filling a vessel drop by drop, there is at last a drop which makes it run over. So in a series of kindness there is, at last, one which makes the heart run over."
SAMUEL JOHNSON

by Amanda Spurling

advice column

Q: I am really upset with my three best friends. No matter what I do to help them or be there for them, they don't seem to do the same for me. I feel used and that these girls are so selfish. They don't seem to care when anyone else is upset or hurting. I really want them to see that I have feelings and I'm not just a taxi service, someone to borrow money from, or someone to lie for them. I don't mind helping them, but I would like them to at least offer to help me or ask how I am every now and then. Am I being selfish to want these things?

A: It is so important in a friendship that each person feels totally supported, loved, and honored. It is also important that we feel that our contribution to the friendship is not taken for granted or abused in any way. It sounds like you are willing to do and be a lot for your friends. But it also sounds like you also feel your generosity is being abused, and that is a concern.

Your story reminds me of another young woman I spoke with recently. She explained how she would literally do everything for her friends—she would buy them beautiful gifts, look after them if they got drunk, give them her brand-new clothes, and even do their assignments or homework. This girl was totally mistreated by her friends. They would even laugh at her and call her names behind her back.

After twelve months, this girl had the most awful self-image. She went from being a fun-loving, popular, confident girl to being timid, depressed, anxious, and suffering severe panic attacks. However, one day, she had had enough and subsequently changed friendship groups. The girls she began to hang out with made her feel like an important, accepted, significant member of their group, and her confidence and zest for life returned.

It's amazing but true that the people we associate with can have a huge effect on our self-esteem. Have you talked to your friends about how you feel? If not, are you willing to? It is so important that you explain to your girlfriends how their actions have affected you. They may be honestly unaware of your feelings and their lack of sensitivity toward you. Sometimes when we are familiar or comfortable with people, we can take their friendship for granted.

If you explain your feelings to your friends and they seem indifferent, you may need to make a choice about whether you want to continue to spend your time with these girls. We are called to be friends, not doormats. If you don't recognize a willingness and significant attempt to change, you may need to move on. Although it may be hard to leave the familiarity of these relationships, anything is better than feeling used or hurt by a friend.

Chelsea's Story

I went to the same school for 12 years. I developed many friendships that came and went and a select few that continued on through the years. I had an amazing group of girlfriends; the five of us were close all through our school years. These relationships were about fun and frivolity. We talked about the hottest boy at school and were more concerned about our own images than looking out for our friends. In this time, the five of us would often switch between who was our best friend in the group, and there were often divisions where we would not speak to each other for weeks. However, we always thought of ourselves as best friends. At the end of tenth grade, we went separate ways, with two of us staying at the same school and the others moving on. It was a sad day, full of tears for each of us, but from that day on, although we promised to stay best friends forever, we saw each other less and less.

I began dating a guy who is now my fiancé. I was fifteen, and while initially we only went out with our group of friends, I spent less and less time just hanging out with the girls. I used our separation as an excuse for why we didn't see each other any more, and I had an attitude that if they didn't call me, why should I call them? I was always very close to my mom, so I felt I didn't need them to guide me, support me, or encourage me. My mom and I had an incredible girl-to-girl friendship, which I will always cherish, but I did begin to realize around the age of seventeen that there was a part of my life that I had neglected. Girlfriends are a gift from God, and I couldn't use these excuses to forsake the opportunity for special female relationships. God showed me that these friendships have been created by Him because girls can relate to each other on an emotional and spiritual level like no one else can.

I did have female friendships, but I felt they did not possess the bond required to discuss what meant most to me: my relationship with God. I began to pray and talk to key people in my life about my desire for a close female friendship. This want for a Christian girlfriend became one of my deepest desires. It often had me in tears, and this was a low point in my life as I felt I was left out of a wonderful sisterhood of women. One day, as I was praying about this need, a verse of Scripture came to my mind: "I will give you the desires of your heart," and I knew at that moment God would provide me with a close girlfriend. He also showed me, however, that I had to change too.

I became proactive in seeking to spend time with my girlfriends. My family and my boyfriend supported me in this and encouraged me to do things with my girlfriends even when I didn't feel like it. For God to answer this prayer, I needed to make time for developing relationships. For another two years, I continued praying in faith and changing how I approached friendships. I knew God did have girlfriends out there for me to develop close relationships with, girls who I would enjoy spending time with and with whom I could share my spiritual journey.

At the end of 2002, I learned that one of my old friends from school was looking for someone to move to Perth with. At the same time, I was looking to move to Perth as I felt it was where God was leading me. We caught up over an iced chocolate (or two), prayed together about the idea, and moved into a unit in South Perth soon after. It was a few months later that I realized my prayer had been answered. I was living with a beautiful girl who had a close relationship with God. We can laugh together, talk about our walk with God, go shopping, cry together, and eat ice cream for dinner!

Since then, I have realized that I have been blessed with two other close girlfriends. One is a beautiful friend from that original group of five. We never lost touch completely, and I realize now that I just did not put in the effort to keep our relationship alive. While we still talk and giggle about boys, these conversations now have a higher purpose. We help each other discover if "he" is the man God has chosen for us, and the advice we give is not centered around our own self-image but on how we can help each other fulfill our God-given potential. I have also been given an amazing sister-in-law. A woman of God full of ambition and a desire to selflessly help others, I can model my life around her own as each day we grow closer in friendship, teaching each other and learning from each other.

From feeling as if I didn't even have one close girlfriend for so many years, I now know I have three! I consider myself extremely blessed by God and continually thank Him for the changes He has made in me and for what I have learned along the journey. He has shown me that it is important for us to be proactive in the way we approach our friendships. They are not to be one-sided, but they require a bit of give-and-take to see them blossom. God has created a union between His girls that cannot be explained, and it may have taken me a while, but I eventually have realized its importance. They are not something we can be blasé about. Our friendships need to be nurtured. Girls need friendship for mentoring and accountability as well as fun and laughter. Girlfriendships need to be cherished. How fantastic to think that when I felt I would never find that close friend, all along God had girls out there planned for me.

girlfriendship

chapter 10: get outta my face
smothering

"Fame is the scentless sunflower, with gaudy crown of gold; But friendship is the breathing rose, with sweets in every fold."
OLIVER WENDEL HOLMES

by Amanda Spurling

Get outta my face
smothering

I've never been a huge fan of horror flicks.

I remember sleeping over at my friend's house, and we decided to watch *Nightmare on Elm Street*. I guess the word *watch* is probably not correct because we were scared witless and peeped out at the movie from under the safety of our pink floral pillows. After "watching" that movie, sleeping became a lot harder to do, and I would desperately force myself to stay awake, fearing Freddy Fingernails would visit me in my dreams.

But there are other movies that have scared me silly. These are movies in the thriller/suspense genre, and one of them was *Single White Female*. Starring Bridget Fonda (as good girl "Allison") and Jennifer Jason Leigh (as bad girl "Heddy"), it starts off harmless enough but soon devolves into a full-on psycho fest. It's all about the bad girl slowly and slyly trying to copy and then steal the good girl's life and identity. On a scale of one to ten, I gave it a big fat TEN on my Creepy Motion Picture Scale!

However, what's truly chilling about this movie is that it's not just make-believe. Copying and trying to assume a friend's identity is a fixation that can ring the death knell on many friendships. Imitation may be the sincerest form of flattery, but it can also be annoying, off-putting, and smothering to the person being imitated.

Although I haven't personally experienced it myself, I have seen friends such as Allison and Heddy who start out as individuals. They have lots in common and get along well. They laugh at the same jokes, enjoy similar music, and even have the same taste in guys. But then, eerily, Heddy begins to echo Allison.

It usually starts off innocently with Heddy regularly complimenting Allison on her clothing style and asking for fashion advice. Allison doesn't mind and is flattered by Heddy looking up to her as a style goddess. But over time, Allison becomes concerned when Heddy starts to dress the same as her, wears the same makeup, gets the same haircut, and even copies her mannerisms.

Heddy becomes unhealthily attached to her friend and demands Allison's undivided time and attention. She calls Allison countless times a day ("just to talk"), makes plans on behalf of Allison, and gets moody and jealous when Allison wants to spend time with other people. Real-life Heddy, unlike celluloid Heddy, is not a psycho or even a bad person; she is, however, insecure and overly dependant on Allison for her sense of security and identity. Allison, on the other hand, just feels smothered and suffocated.

For a friendship to flourish, it's important to respect each other's space. One of my favorite things to do is just to simply hang with my friends. But too much time and familiarity can put people off, so it's important to develop different circles of friends and interests.

Although Aly and I are best friends, we don't see each other every day (very hard to do now that we live in different cities!). We don't even talk every day, and there are interests we don't share. One of these things is going to the markets. I love the markets! I love the smell, the color, the busyness, and the hustle and bustle of the markets. But the markets make Aly feel like puking, and for her, hanging out with me does not include going to them. So instead, I go to the markets with my close friend Amanda. We can spend hours just looking around and getting totally lost in the atmosphere. We like to touch and smell everything, and we usually leave with some great bargains ($10 silk embroidered Chinese slippers, yeah!). So Aly is my anti-market friend and Amanda is my pro-market friend. I love them both, and we share a variety of interests.

It's also important for me to just enjoy spending time with myself. And even though this is a book on friendships with others, it's vital to know who you are so you can give your best to your friends. Spending time with yourself doesn't need to be boring and bland; in fact it can be great fun. Take some solo time out and read a great book or mag, listen to your favorite music, and here's something to totally scare you: Go to the movies...by yourself! You'll be surprised that when you're alone, you don't have to be lonely.

John Leonard said, "It takes a long time to grow an old friend," but too much time together and not giving each other space will stunt and strangle a friendship. So give each other space and time, and allow the friendship to blossom.

A **friend** may well be reckoned the **masterpiece** of nature.

RALPH WALDO EMERSON

by Amanda Spurling

advice column

Do you feel constricted or claustrophobic in a certain friendship? Many young women feel this way but do not know if they are just being ungrateful or unsupportive.

Here are some danger signs of smothering relationships:

1. The very thing that attracts one personality to another initially is the very thing that becomes smothering, driving the victim away. This could be the other person's flattery, strong assertive nature, constant desire to be around her friend, charm, or confidence. If any of these traits are used negatively or become obsessive, demanding, and confronting, they can lead to resentment and, in some cases, the person feels smothered or stalked.

2. The smothering person denies any problem, refuses to talk about the victim's feelings, or starts to become intimidating in the relationship if her motives are questioned. Unless there is a conscious effort to eliminate these obstacles or flaws in the relationship, then relational strain will occur. Sometimes people who are obsessively smothering in relationships have to seek professional counseling to identify the source of their relational issues and find ways to balance their emotions.

3. The smothering party finds it almost impossible to be without the other person and becomes manipulative, jealous, or angry if her friend expresses a desire for less interaction or tries to end the friendship. This is a very real issue for some people. They are so obsessed with a relationship that they find it almost impossible to be without their friend and cannot see that their behavior is offensive or disturbing. It doesn't mater how much the relationship is hurting them or their friend—anything is better than being alone. In extreme cases, medical or psychological help and/or police intervention is required.

Tara's Story

I guess I could say that, at some point, I was a smothering kind of friend. Due to a lack of interest in me at home, I found refuge in my group of Christian friends. I have wonderful friends, who are genuinely interested in me and my walk with God. I had one friend in particular who I went to church with and who was my "best friend," and we used to hang out all the time after school, at church, and on the weekends. We were genuine friends who really cared for each other and wanted the best for each other.

After a few years, some stuff happened in my life that led me to question everything about my walk with God and why on earth I believed what I did. I was wracked with guilt and just dying for someone to love me and tell me that everything would be OK. This poor best friend of mine then had to deal with me relying on her to stay afloat, and it really dragged our friendship down. It wasn't totally one-way. I am a very generous friend and would do anything for someone who needed something, but I just wasn't an emotional or spiritual equal who could help share problems—I would just dump them and cry for help. One day it came to the point where my friend had to tell me that she couldn't deal with this kind of friendship anymore—that it weighed her down and wasn't healthy—and I was left alone.

It almost killed me. I had really clung on to this particular friend and relied on her to nurture me in my Christian walk and to be there for me whenever I needed her. I know now that it was totally unhealthy for her as well as for me. I had placed so much significance on her input in my life and the way God could talk to me through her that I had lost focus of who God is—our best friend.

All He wants to do is be our best friend and talk to us constantly. He's there to share our burden and bring us joy. He's the one who knows us inside out and wants to wipe away our tears and help us to be more than we ever dreamed of. Being such a smothering friend at that time has made me reassess the place of friends in my life, and now I to run to God rather than straight to my friends.

girlfriendship

chapter 11: handle with care

trust broken

"No soul is desolate as long as there is a human being for whom it can feel trust and reverence."
GEORGE ELIOT

by Amanda purling

Handle with care
trust broken

I remember recently reading the most amazing story of courage.

It was about two girlfriends, Anne and Debi, who had gone mountain bike riding in Wilderness Park, California, never realizing that they were about to experience an ordeal that would test their friendship to the extreme.

While biking along a well-worn track, Anne was suddenly attacked by a large male mountain lion. Two guys riding their bikes nearby heard Debi screaming the chilling words, "My friend is getting eaten by a mountain lion!"

When the guys rushed to the aid of the girls, they felt instant terror. They saw the lion with its mouth engulfing Anne's entire head and dragging her off the bike track into the bush. Debi, however, had courageously grabbed hold of Anne's leg in a life-and-death tug-of-war, determined not to let her friend die. Debi yelled for the guys to start throwing rocks at the lion. The first rock hit the lion in the leg, but it didn't even flinch or let go of its prey. The guys threw a second rock. This time it hit the lion squarely behind its head and it let go of Anne.

Paramedics quickly arrived on the scene, and Anne was airlifted to a nearby hospital where she survived and was treated for severe lacerations to her face and neck. When interviewed about their harrowing experience, Debi said, "It was pretty much adrenaline. It's not something you train for. I think you either have it in your instincts or you don't."[1]

The guys described Debi as incredibly brave, considering that the mountain lion could have easily let go of Anne and swiped Debi with its paw. They said, "Debi was fearless. She was basically going face-to-face with this mountain lion saying, 'You're not taking my friend. Dead or alive, she is coming with me.'"[2]

WOW! I don't know about you, but I'd love to have a friend like that! Someone you can trust with your very life and know that when stuff hits the fan or you find yourself trapped in the lion's mouth, she won't let you go down without a fight.

But the stuff of great friendships is also what can cause great friendships to seriously stuff up! That stuff is made up of a five-letter word...TRUST. And trust is only proven when it's tested. In the case of Anne and Debi, it was tested in the most harrowing of circumstances. But in most cases, trust is tested in the little things and in the everyday.

It's very rare that any of us will find ourselves battling lions to save our friend, but we will find ourselves in situations where we can choose to defend our friend when someone is gossiping about them.

Trust between friends is a foundation that is built up over time, but cracks in that foundation can easily appear by doing the wrong thing or not doing the right thing.

Some of the causes of the cracks are:

Being two-faced
This means saying one thing to your friend but deceiving her behind her back. I've known girls who have come across as all sweet and innocent but secretly they've connived to ruin their friend's reputation, steal her job, or two-time with her boyfriend.

Being a blabber-mouth
There's nothing worse than having a friend who promises not to tell anyone your confidential information but then can't help herself, and before you know it, people who hardly know you know all about your personal issues.

Being everyone's friend
It's incredibly hurtful to have a friend who doesn't defend you when others bad-mouth you or, even worse, joins in the bad-mouthing. This is usually the type of friend who wants to be everyone's friend and doesn't have the backbone to be a friend that really counts.

When trust is broken in a friendship, it can make us feel incredibly angry, hurt, betrayed, and isolated. We wonder whether we can ever trust again, and we put up walls around our hearts, giving them time to heal but also ensuring they won't easily be broken again. Over time, usually the friendship is able to be salvaged and grow even stronger. But sadly, there are other times when we are unable to pull down the walls that allow us to again be vulnerable, and the friendship is irreparably damaged.

When it all comes down to it, the issue of trust in girlfriendship is fraught with challenges, potholes, and obstacles (and the occasional rampaging lion). And how we choose to strengthen or damage this crucial friendship ingredient is up to us. But when trust is strong between friends, it gives us the liberty to dare to be ourselves. And there is nothing more liberating than knowing that someone knows the real you and yet still chooses to be your friend.

Jean De La BruFre said, "Two persons cannot long be friends if they cannot forgive each other's little failings." And that also means making the hard choice to trust again when trust has been broken.

I do not wish to treat friendships daintily, but with the roughest courage. When they are real, they are not glass threads or frostwork, but the solidest thing we know.

RALPH WALDO EMERSON

advice column

Q: My best friend and I have known each other all our lives. Our moms were friends before we were born. We have always been there for each other. However, three months ago my best friend did something really hurtful, and I feel totally betrayed by her. I can no longer look at her the same, and even though I know she feels really sorry for what she did, I have not been able to forgive her. Please help me. I don't want to lose her friendship, but how can I ever trust her again?

A: The feeling of betrayal is a powerful emotion. When someone we love hurts us, intentionally or otherwise, we can feel empty, numb, sick, confused, disappointed, or angry—even a mixture of all these emotions. All these feelings are normal. However, our recovery and the rebuilding of the friendship is dependent upon how we respond to these emotions. In this situation, it seems that you are at a point where you recognize that, for your friendship to continue, you must see some merit to forgiving your friend and moving on from this breach of trust.

While you may still feel quite distrusting of your friend at the moment, you may find that over time you are able to forgive and trust her. Time often helps put into perspective what has happened. Was this incident really worth giving up a lifetime friendship? Your friend has shown remorse for her actions and therefore deserves a chance to redeem herself.

One of the most liberating forces on the planet is forgiveness. If you can find it in your heart to forgive your friend and begin to give her opportunities to rebuild your trust in her, you may find an even sweeter, stronger friendship evolves out of this situation. If you are unable to forgive, you give room in your heart for bitterness to remain, and that will ruin any chance of you moving on in a hurry. Even if you retain the friendship, you will not be able to celebrate and enjoy your friend because you will be too busy remembering all the bad things she has done to you.

Even though betrayal hurts, it is certainly not the end of a relationship, unless you choose for it to be. You will need to be honest with your friend as you continue to rebuild your trust in her, and she will need to understand that it will take time for the hurt to heal. But if you are both willing to commit to rebuilding the friendship, and if you are able to forgive your friend, you may find in time that it is the best decision you could have made.

You will need to be gracious, and your friend will need to prove herself. But the grace is on the other side of your decision to forgive. What have you got to lose?

Jess's Story

When I was first asked to write this, I had to sit down and think about what my girlfriends really mean to me and how important they are. They are ultimately my support system and accountability partners who have kept me on the straight and narrow and been faithful with the friendship we have shared. God has always blessed me in the way of friendships, not in the sense that I had millions of friends but in that my relationships with each individual taught me something about who I am and who I wanted to become.

My closest friends have always been there to listen and believe in me, and we have supported each other through the significant issues, and also the not so significant. I have an awesome group of school friends who have helped me to recognize that my dreams are so much closer than they often seemed to be and who constantly remind me of my potential. They have sown into my life with little recognition of the cost, which may have been in the form of very little sleep or dropping everything to help me out, and I thank God so much for those girls because they have helped me grow and are continuing to help me grow into the woman I was created to be.

Unfortunately, my life has not always been as beautiful as it is becoming. Throughout elementary school, I had a lot of friends, that is, up until fourth grade when my "best friend" and I began hanging out as just the two of us and basically separated ourselves from the other kids. Eventually, she stopped coming to "our place," and I found out that she had become friends with the popular group behind my back. This one incident made me put up walls around my heart and my life, not allowing anyone to come too close to me for the fear of being hurt again. It also made me extremely self-conscious and caused me to always worry about what people thought of me.

Things looked up again for a while, until I went to high school. I had these two "best friends" in eighth and ninth grade, and the three of us were incredibly close until one day (for a reason that I can't even remember), we began to have these intense fights, which took up almost two years of our lives. I won't go into detail, but what occurred caused me to fortify the walls I had built many years before, and I kept people at arm's length for a long time. This made it more difficult for me to make friends since I would not open up to people; and it took a very long time to get to know me as a person. Although I look back and it seemed to be such a waste of time and effort, the year would have hurt me so much more if I had not learned to rely on God. My trust in God was forced to grow significantly during that year, as I had no one else to turn to because I had pushed everyone away. I will always remember now that God is my closest friend.

It has taken me quite a few years (I am a slow learner) to slowly break down the walls in my life. It has taken the friendship of many awesome, beautiful people to help me begin to trust and put my feelings back on the line, and it is totally worth it! I have learned to change. I am no longer that little girl who seemed to have it all together but had created so many walls that she blocked all emotions from reaching her heart. I can now do simple things like talk about my problems with other people, without the fear of them hurting me or laughing at my pain. And with God's help, I can now cry. This sounds so simple, but for me, the girl who could not cry and express the pain she felt because she had taught herself not to, it was a massive step. Even now, I often find it hard to verbalize my feelings because of little incidents in my past. I now realize that true friendships blossom if a person is not willing to put her heart on the line. Although many people may hurt you, you will never know what kind of amazing friendships you will experience if you don't learn to trust.

girlfriendship

chapter 12: when the claws come out
emotional aggression

"Friendship is one of the sweetest joys of life. Many might have failed beneath the bitterness of their trial had they not found a friend."

CHARLES HADDON SPURGEON

by Amanda Spurling

When the claws come out
emotional aggression

If you were to describe your friendships with your closest girlfriends, what words would you use? Honest? Superficial? Genuine? Two-faced? Supportive? Honoring? Trusting? Hopefully most of you would be able to say that you enjoy strong friendships where you feel comfortable being yourself and expressing your feelings and opinions without judgment, and your friend makes you feel totally loved and genuinely supported.

No matter how strong our relationships are with other females, studies have shown that women have a very unique way of letting each other know when they are unhappy, displeased, upset, or angry at one another.

One of the major issues I have encountered as I have talked with young women about their friendships with other females is a phenomenon known as emotional aggression. This phenomenon explains the way in which females use emotional responses, either knowingly or subconsciously, to let another girl know that she is no longer in her good book! Emotional aggression includes cattiness, moodiness, tantrums, and intimidation.

Cattiness

This is when a girl is verbally aggressive toward another girl—deliberately saying hurtful things or criticizing her dress, actions, choices, appearance, or anything else she knows will be upsetting. Cattiness is not subtle; it is a deliberate and vocal attempt by the "cat" to let the other person know that she is not acceptable, not welcome, or not up to scratch (pardon the pun!).

Moodiness

Who hasn't experienced the awful fate of walking into the black cloud of another female's "subtle rage"? Moodiness is the emotional repression of anger, hurt, or frustration that shows itself in sulky, silent standoffs. The problem is that moodiness is unproductive in dealing with issues or upsets. Moodiness is commonly a nonverbal act, so although the body language expresses great indignation, when the moody girl is asked what the cause of her mood is, the response is usually either "nothing" or "if you don't know, I'm not telling you." This makes it very difficult for the actual issue to be dealt with. Usually a number of minutes, hours, or days must pass (depending on severity of mood) to allow the dark cloud to disappear. Often the moody person will come back hours later, bright and chirpy again, or will suddenly put on their brightest smile when a non-offending person walks by. Very confusing.

Tantrums

Some girls' dramatic flair for tantrums and melodrama is so great their display would rival any Academy Award nominee. Those of us not blessed with such tantrum talent can only sit and marvel at their nerve, their gusto, and their ability to turn on the tears at a moment's notice. I have seen girls storm out of restaurants, fall in a dishevelled heap in the middle of female restrooms, refuse to come out of bedrooms or bathrooms, sob uncontrollably, and scream until their faces became distorted beyond recognition. These are girls who are used to getting their own way and will do whatever it takes to get what they want. The worst thing is when they accidentally lock themselves in the bathroom. Fire and emergency departments aren't very understanding of hissy-fit-induced call-outs, even if your world really is falling apart!

Intimidation

This is the most serious of all types of emotional aggression and can range from bullying to blackmail. Any behavior that is threatening or that intentionally endangers the safety of another human being is completely unacceptable. Bullying is when we threaten others with penalty, endangerment, "accidents," or terrorizing incidents if they don't comply with our demands. It can include physical intimidation or violence in extreme cases.

Blackmail is a more subtle form of intimidation, although it can be just as devastating. This is when a person is given verbal or written threats to their safety, reputation, or well-being if they do not comply with the demands of the offender. Emotional blackmail is when we deliberately try to persuade a change or desired effect on a person by making promises or threats that affect the person's relationships or reputation. This is called *coercion,* and it affects the emotional and relational security of the victim.

Obviously these are the negative aspects of girlfriendship. We don't ever expect that our beautiful, fun-filled, honoring relationships could ever be subject to these nasties. However, it is important to know that emotional aggression is a phenomenon that many girls experience and to recognize its various forms so that our relationships are not threatened or destroyed by it.

by Amanda Spurling

"Oh, the comfort—
the inexpressible comfort of feeling safe
with a person—
having neither to weigh thoughts
nor measure words,
but pouring them all right out,
just as they are,
chaff and grain together;
certain that a faithful hand
will take and sift them,
keep what is worth keeping,
and then with the breath of kindness
blow the rest away."
DINAH MARIA MULOCK CRAIK

advice column

Q: I am in deep trouble. My friends have disowned me and won't even answer my calls or letters. Recently I accused one of them of flirting with my boyfriend while I was away on vacation. Unfortunately, I was unable to control myself and called my friend every name I could think of and tried to make her life miserable. I even told some of my friends that the next time I saw her, I would hit her. Although I didn't mean it, everyone believed I would do it, and now no one wants to talk to me. My boyfriend later told me it was him who did the flirting, but I was not angry with him even though I know I should have been. I need help, but I have no one to talk to about my anger problem or the way I reacted. I don't know who I can trust. What should I do?

A: There are two issues here. First of all, you have an inability to deal appropriately with feelings of anger, hurt, or betrayal. Even if your friend had been the one flirting, your response was still inappropriate and signals a high degree of explosive anger. Human beings were made with the ability to feel angry; this is not a bad thing. What is problematic is when we respond aggressively or without restraint on these feelings.

The second concern I have is that you do not seem able to talk about your feelings with someone you trust. I wonder if you would have acted out in this manner if you had someone you could have articulated your feelings to and even explained what you wanted to do or say to your friend. I am almost convinced that you would have handled the situation differently if you had been able to talk with a trusted confidante about how this alarming accusation even began to be formulated in your thoughts. "Accountability" is what we term this kind of relationship. It's a relationship where you can honestly and openly share how you feel in a safe and appropriate way.

Accountability means that you have to allow yourself to divulge information about yourself and your life that only you are aware of, and then you have to give another person permission to speak into your world, truthfully and openly. Accountable relationships give you the freedom to truly express how you feel when things happen that you don't like or understand. But they also help you to make right choices about the things you can and should change.

Here are some ideas on developing accountability:

1. Talk to another girl before you respond

Stick with girls who have had a little bit more life experience than you have. They will speak wisdom and encouragement into your life but will also be pretty sensitive to what it is like to go through the issues you are facing. This could be a teacher, a sister, a mother, a counselor, a friend's mom, or a youth worker. Whoever you choose, make sure she is your first point of contact before you make any decisions on how you are going to respond to a situation.

2. Find someone you feel completely safe with

Trust is a massive factor when you are exposing your deepest (and sometimes your darkest!) feelings or needs to someone else. You need to be able to relax in this person's company and be you, not feel like you are in a therapy session where the counselor is distant, removed, or inaccessible. The person should be someone you connect with on a personal level but doesn't necessarily need to be a close friend. In fact, sometimes it can be easier if it is someone who is not a close acquaintance simply because they tend to be a bit more objective in their counsel. For some people, counselors and anger therapists are great, but these can be expensive. Check your local youth center, church, or health center or consult your local community center for assistance and information. There are also specialized anger management courses available if required.

Above everything, accountable relationships prevent us from living life alone, even in the company of others. They help us to stay safe in our journey of life and not to wander into dangerous territory. A good friend, confidante, or counselor can help you identify some reasons for why you reacted the way you did and help you put some preventative measures in place. I trust you will seek out someone you can rely on to explore your concerns with.

Gina's Story

During my years in elementary school and high school, I had some very impacting experiences with friendships. Some I can never forget. I was blessed with some really good friendships in my senior high school years. I really believe that God was making up to me what I had missed out on in elementary school and junior high.

You see, I had a really rough time with friendships from around the age of 10 to 15. I went through some really hurtful and painful experiences with girls in my class, who were supposedly my friends. I desired to be liked by everyone and to be named one of the popular girls. Every girl wants to be popular in school, but that's never up to her to decide. The girls I called my "friends" were nice to me sometimes, but most of the time they were catty and mean to me and talked about me behind my back. There was a ringleader of the group (who was the popular, influential one), and if you were liked by her, you were liked by everyone. I was not liked very much by her because I wasn't cool enough. I wasn't hip or worldly enough for the group, so I just hung back and didn't join in on the conversations. Whatever I said didn't have any importance, and I certainly didn't dress to their standards.

One particular girl in the group, who was very insecure about herself, would constantly mock me and put me down in front of the other girls. In doing this, she managed to lift herself up and gain acceptance from the others. There was one game that was played every lunch hour: handball. It went from being just a fun sporty game to a game of popularity. The rule was that the girl who brought the ball to school had the power to choose who could play and who couldn't. Of course this one girl, who loved to put me down, would bring the ball every day and never let me play. She was using the game as what I call a "power play" to control others. She would say, with a mean tone in her voice, "Everyone can play...except Gina." The other girls never defended me, so I sat out and watched, feeling very hurt and rejected.

Another hurtful experience that I will never forget was with the same group of girls. Just when I thought we were all starting to get along, they turned on me. They all formed a little huddle, leaving me standing on the outside by myself, and they drew straws to kick me out of the group. The girl who got the shortest straw broke the news to me.

I went through a lot of other experiences like these throughout school, and it was not fun. Since those times, I have pushed the memories to the back of my mind, but writing this has made me realize I have not forgiven these girls for the trouble they caused me. So I know I need to forgive them and then move on with my life.

Even though I have had some tough times with girlfriendships, God really has blessed me now with some wonderful and refreshing girlfriendships. All my friends are powering on for God and are some of the most amazing people I've ever met. We all have a heart to serve God and to support each other in good and bad times. I am now experiencing blossoming friendships because Jesus is the center of it all. He is the key to great girlfriendships!

girlfriendship

chapter 13: let the games begin

competition between girls

"*You just reminded me of what's really important in life: friends...best friends.*"

FRIED GREEN TOMATOES

by Amanda Spurling

Let the games begin
competition between girls

Ever since I was a young girl in elementary school, I dreaded the weekly P.E. (physical education) class.

I was never any good at sports. In fact, I was embarrassingly tragic and usually made a complete fool of myself, but that certainly didn't stop me from persistently fantasizing about one day competing in the Olympic games.

Yes, you could say I was a bit of a dreamer (and probably still am), and when it came to sports, I was the biggest daydreamer of them all. I was utterly useless in reality but a gold medalist in my head. And in my space-cadet fantasy world, I could compete with the best of them in athletics, diving, gymnastics, horseback riding, and especially the crème de la crème of sports...synchronized swimming!

Sadly, even though I left elementary school many eons ago, I still find myself occasionally drifting off to the Olympic dreamscape whenever *Wide World of Sports* is shown on the television. But I'm usually jolted back to reality by the sports fanatics around me frothing at the mouth and yelling at the coach or the competitor in TV-land. I will never understand why people get so worked up about sports, but being the considerate person I am, I always offer them my well-worn trusty piece of advice: "Chill out...it's only a stupid game."

And when it comes to the day-to-day, many of us also view life as a game.

We see other people as competitors; teachers and parents as our coaches and umpires; the "popular crowd" as the winners; and the "weirdos, nerds, geeks, and tech-heads" as the losers. We live the motto of the reality show *Survivor* by competing to outwit, outplay, and outlast all others, to claim the million dollar booty and the title of sole survivor. And we keep reminding ourselves that "nobody remembers second best...it's the winner who takes all."

But life is not a game to outshine others, and when we mistakenly live it as one, we lose.

Girl versus girl is a no-win scenario. By competing with our Cinderella-girlfriend for popularity, success, status, opportunities, attention, and that all-elusive bachelor, we become the ugly stepsisters of jealousy, rivalry, and comparison. Those who should be our closest allies and confidants become our competitors, and although we may publicly wish them well, secretly we're conniving to be the one to receive that precious, long-stemmed rose!

The main reason female rivalry is rife in our society is because we define ourselves unrealistically and therefore compete for things that are immaterial: dress size, breast size, wardrobe size, phone size, guy by our side, shoes on our feet, highlights in our hair, and how many text messages messages we receive.

But in defining our worth by these superficial price tags, we deprive ourselves of what is really important in life: friends...girlfriends. When we label ourselves, we also label others and in doing so eventually have to come to the conclusion that someone is always going to have a better label, and the question is, What price will we pay for it?

Author Rachael Oakes-Ash wrote that, "Female competition is a taboo topic. It's covert, rarely spoken about in public but it exists....The girlfriend who is as thin as a toothpick and forever parading her flat midriff while pinching imaginary fat and complaining of her size. Or the single white female who buys the same clothes as you and has her eyes on your man....Female competition keeps corporations in the money as fear keeps us consuming—fear we'll be left out, excluded, too fat, not thin enough, not young enough, not pretty enough, not rich enough, simply not enough."[3]

Sadly, comparison and competition make us feel empty on the inside. Although we may sometimes "win" our little games, it is a hollow victory. It robs us of being connected with other girls in a way that is real and fulfilling.

Within all of us there is a longing to be known, loved, understood, and befriended. By taking off the cracked glasses that view other girls as rivals, foes, and challengers, we give ourselves the chance to see them simply as friends and allow them to complement our lives.

Girlfriendship is what adds true value to our existence. It opens up our worlds and enriches our lives with unique experiences, blessed moments, and treasured memories.

The simple truth is...we can't have our friends and compete with them too.

A **blessed** thing it is to have a **friend**.

CHARLES KINGSLEY

by Amanda Spurling

advice column

Q: I don't know how to make my friend see that she doesn't have to compete with me. I love her to death, but I am getting so frustrated at her constant need to outdo me. Lately I feel like she can't even talk to me without telling me how good she is at something or how bad my skin is or how unfashionable I am. To be honest, I am not interested in having a friendship that is measured by who is or does better. Please help me get through to her!

A: It sounds like it is very important to your friend that others (especially yourself) see her as significant or worthy of attention. Perhaps you might want to investigate the reasons that your friend wants you to see her this way. Does she feel she needs to put you down in order to feel better about herself? Perhaps your friend doesn't recognize that her criticisms are not as constructive as she thinks. They may actually be more about her insecurities than your limitations. In many cases, when good friends are competitive with one another, there is an underlying current of jealousy, resentment, insecurity, or feeling devalued.

Be honest with your friend. Let her know that you have noticed her behavior toward you has changed lately, and ask her if she is aware of these changes. If she has been unaware of her actions, this will be the perfect opportunity for her to take inventory of where she is and why she has responded to you in a competitive way. If this has been an ongoing pattern, you may need to alert your friend as to when you initially began to see her competitiveness toward you. Perhaps there was an emotional or relational trigger point that has yet to be identified by your friend.

Often competitiveness is only a symptom of a greater threat to a person's emotional or mental state. Perhaps your friend is angry or upset or hurt about an element of your friendship, and although she has not overtly stated it, she is using competition to feel like she has the upperhand in the relationship. Perhaps she is unsettled about another issue in her life, and this is her way of venting her feelings.

The only way you will know why your friend is behaving this way is to have the courage to ask her. Be gentle, but let her know your concerns for her and the friendship. Be specific. Use examples such as: "Yesterday, when you said my skin was looking pretty bad, I felt a bit hurt. Were you aware of how it may have sounded?" Or, "I have been finding lately that our friendship seems a bit competitive. Have you noticed any competition between us?" This way, you are not "blaming" her or finding fault, but merely stating the specific reasons for your hurt and outlining your concerns for the friendship. Above all, be patient with your friend and make sure she knows that your concerns are genuine. Resolving underlying issues is a huge part of growing and maturing a friendship. Hopefully your friend will see this too!

Te-neele's Story

I look around in my room, and everywhere are photos, letters, pictures, notes, and memories. Countless moments worth remembering. Funnily enough, not one of those memories is just of me, alone—they all have my friends or family sharing in the memory. As I look at these memories, I cannot help but smile. Each photo holds such a valued place in my heart—each person played a part in my life, and I played a part in theirs.

There was a time, however, when I smiled in the photos while inside I was unhappy. I was insecure about who I was, and I, like so many other people, just wanted to fit in, but more so, to be popular. It was in this time that I developed an eating disorder. I thought most of the popular girls were thin, therefore to be more popular, I needed to be thin. I deceived a lot of people, most of whom are with me in the photos on my wall.

It wasn't until I finished school that I saw any improvement in my self-image. I went straight into Bible college, unaware of the incredible ride ahead. Over the year, I met the most incredible people who poured out their love and acceptance over me. I have only just finished my first year of Bible college, and the lessons I have learned go so far beyond what can be tested and examined at the end of a term. I learned lifelong lessons about myself, and what friendship is, from the beautiful girls I shared the college experience with.

I learned to remain confident in who I was, even in the times when my friends and family weren't able to lift my confidence. I began to understand that it is not the duty of other people to make me feel good about myself, but it is a choice I have to make. And it is something that requires me to depend on God alone for my self-worth rather than measuring it by who I am with or by the nice things others say about me.

I have also learned that if I want true friendship, I need to be a true friend—that if I want people to listen to me, I have to genuinely listen to them and hear their hearts.

I've learned that if I want to be accepted, I need to accept other people and love them exactly the way they are.

It wasn't just the people in college who taught me. I was lead and directed by so many people. I learned to put myself in the position of others (instead of judging them). It was from these people that I began to understand that life is meant to be fun, but we have to make that choice. The people around me are so humble that I have learned that humility is not staying quiet nor is it shrugging off compliments; humility is knowing who you are in Christ, accepting who you are in Christ, and being who you are in Christ.

Having come to know such incredible people, I was forced to look at my older friendships and to ask myself if they were healthy relationships where a burden was shared, or if they were friendships where a burden was loaded onto one person alone. There is a difference between being friends and giving someone a piggyback through life, and there were times when I found that I needed to change. I now understand that while it is not the duty of a friend to keep my spirits high, support and encouragement should come from a friend and should also be given to a friend.

Finally, I have learned that pretending to be someone else, someone seemingly better, will never make me happy. I have to be myself. I realize now that I don't have to be better, look better, be funnier...nothing is an improvement to being myself. Someone once said, "The people who are always pretending to be someone they aren't, and are always wearing a mask, are the people who are nervous all the time." This acts as a continual reminder for me that I will never be comfortable with myself if I'm trying to be someone else.

The memories that cover my bedroom walls still never fail to make me smile. They act as a reminder that my friendships should never again contain the deception they once did, the deception that I gave out. True friendship requires total honesty. The photos tell me that true friends will accept me and love me unconditionally and that I should do the same in return.

girlfriendship

Background text (repeated throughout):
forget. True friends are hard to find, difficult to leave, and impossible to forget. True friends are hard to find, difficult to leave, and impossible to forget. True friends are hard to find, difficult to leave, and impossible to forget.

chapter 14: priceless
true friendship

"True friends are hard to find, difficult to leave, and impossible to forget."
AMANDA KUNKLE

by Amanda Spurling

Priceless
true friendship

She's gone.

As I sit and write these words, Mary is flying away to a new city, a new life, a new world. I didn't go to the airport this morning. She knows how I feel about good-byes. I'm at my worst at airports—all that farewell trauma in the atmosphere. Daddies with tears in their eyes as children whisper, "Please don't go." Couples steal just one more embrace as the ominous final boarding call signals the end. Best friends promise to write every week. Toddlers with faces planted against viewing deck windows watch their grannies fly toward the horizon as they sadly reassure teddy that "she'll be back soon." No, I'm afraid airports just don't agree with me.

We had lunch together yesterday. It was better that way. No trauma. No running mascara. No tear-streaked faces. Very grown up. We both held it together pretty well. It wasn't till I got home that I started to sob like a baby.

She's gone.

It just doesn't feel real. My best friend left town today, and I'm not quite sure what I will do without her. Who will I talk to? Who will I share my secrets with? Who will I laugh with? Who will I dream with? Who will see me at my worst and love me anyway? Who will give me much-needed advice? Who will I eat chocolate muffins with? Who will I do nothing with? Who will I shop with?!

I want to make her come back. I want to get on the next plane to Sydney. I want to see her new world and be part of her new adventure. But I know that I can't. Not today. One day, maybe, but not today.

I know I need to trust that our friendship will span the miles, that our hearts will still be knit together forever. I need to believe that, although life will be strange for a little while, it will still be rich, and our friendship will grow even stronger through the years.

She's gone.

As we said our good-byes yesterday, I knew things wouldn't be the same. But today as I sit and write these words, I know that things don't have to be so different. Ours is not a frail friendship. It is a bond built on implicit trust. And that will never change.

I have seen Mary fiercely defend my reputation, my honor, my character, my motives. She has fought for me, even when I was not worthy of such a fight. She has been my advocate. She has believed in me without question, without reservation, without exception.

But today she is gone.

Now I have to trust another time. I have to take a deep breath and jump off the cliff. I have to trust that once again I will be caught and carried by the wings of friendship— wings that span the miles and that will never let us fall.

Six years ago a girl walked into my life and helped me trust again. Today she got on a plane and left. And though I am sad, I am not without hope. True friendship is not about geography. It's not about proximity. It's about solid trust and creating moments that somehow become your shared history—a history you never forget.

To be able to have an open, honest forum in which to express your deepest feelings and secret longings is to be given a beautiful gift. The knowledge that another human being accepts you for who you are and doesn't divulge your precious and personal feelings to anyone else gives you a sense of true freedom in your friendships. It is this trust factor that is truly vital to friendships.

Yes, she is gone—but never too far away.

Friendships are like precious jewels—
We treasure them.
We despair when they are lost or broken.
We love them even as they age.
If looked after they continually sparkle.
They are valuable beyond replacement.

ALYSON PASSAUER

advice column

Q: I have just returned to my hometown after living overseas for two years. In that time I was corresponding regularly with a close friend of mine. Although I have seen her a few times since I have returned, she seems to be trying to avoid me. I have also heard from other girls in our town that my friend is keeping her distance from me. I am very confused. Our relationship has always been an honest one, but I am scared to confront her and ask her what is wrong. What should I do?

A: Nothing breaks down a friendship quicker than relying on other people's evidence or hearsay. Third parties are not always the best people to get information from concerning relationships that are dear and precious to you. The only way you will know if anything really has changed between you and your friend is to ask her. Make time to take her out for coffee or go for a walk together. Let her know that you have noticed at times she feels uncomfortable around you and that you would really like her to tell you what is bothering her. Let her know that you are not angry or upset but a little bit confused, especially since your relationship seemed good when she was writing to you.

Perhaps something has occurred in the life of your friend that she can't talk about. It could be something totally unrelated to your friendship, but she may feel that you know her so well that you will guess her secret. You may need to assure her of your support and that she can trust you. This will at least give her an opportunity to talk if she needs to. Nothing solidifies a friendship better than when friends prove they are trustworthy by keeping each other's secrets confidential.

You will need to have the courage to ask your friend whether she is upset and, if so, whether you can help in any way. Let her know that you are available to listen without judgment, and although you have been away for a while, you still want to be her confidante.

If your friend does indicate that she has a problem with you personally, or that she truly does feel strange having you back in town, then this is a different matter. You say that you and your friend have always been totally honest with one another, so you will need to ask your friend to be honest once again and explain to you directly why she feels the way she does. You may want to tell her what you have heard from others and ask her to verify if these conversations have any truth to them. If she truly does feel differently toward you or does want to keep her distance, you may have to accept that the relationship has changed, and despite your best efforts, you cannot keep a friendship alive all by yourself.

Conversely, your friend may simply be getting used to having you around again, and although it may take time to rekindle your old familiarity and friendship, she may be more than willing to do this. Human beings can be strange creatures—any form of change can sometimes throw us off-kilter. Sometimes it just takes a little while for the dust to settle on new situations, and we can react in surprising ways. So talk to your friend. Be as patient as you can be. Your friend may just surprise you again—this time in a good way!

Sabina's Story

I believe that friendships are very special. The good and the bad friendships help us to become the people we are. Through their love, encouragement, and support, friends teach us, help us to set goals, and motivate us to achieve them. Through hurts and arguments, they strengthen us. Yet friends also soften our hearts and show us how to love when we have forgotten.

Friendships are something that should be treasured forever. Without friends, we would not be who we are....I would not be the person I am today without them. I know that for a fact, as I know who I was before and compare that to who I am now. Yes, when I was younger, I had "friendship issues" because my mother passed away when I was young. I pushed away those I cared about and hid my hurt behind a mask. I kept everything I was feeling to myself and pretended to be something I wasn't.

I remember in first grade there were these two awesome girls, Sally and Jessica. I knew these girls for a few months before my mother passed away, and when everyone else tiptoed around me and treated me differently, they were themselves. We played together, and on rare occasions, we fought with each other, but I learned a lot from these girls over the years. Like Sally...she could never hurt anything. She was always kind and gentle. If you squished an ant, she would cry. So I learned how to not squish ants. And I learned that if you eat ice cream really fast, you get a brain freeze. In fourth grade, Sally and I had an ice cream eating competition. I was in too much pain to actually remember who won. And Jess, she was always happy, always had something nice to say. She was kind and was always there with a shoulder to cry on. I learned from her not to let people make me feel smaller than I am. These two girls have been there for me through thick and thin, and even though we won't hear from each other for months, we still share this special bond.

Beginning high school was one of the most difficult changes I had to make—moving from a Christian school to a public school where I had to make a whole new bunch of friends. That was when I realized how important friendships are. I was surrounded by friends and then left with just one because I argued with their beliefs and was rude when they had something to say about mine. This went on for almost a year, and I realized I was being stubborn, so I apologized. I am glad I did because the friends I made in high school, even though we share different beliefs, taught me some important lessons. My closest friend, Lisa, taught me to value other's beliefs, because you can learn a lot from them. Even though she taught me a lot, I have to admit that she was not exactly the best influence on me. I can't blame her for my mistakes since I made those choices that drew me away from God. Together we were two party girls... don't get me wrong, I wasn't **that** bad. I didn't do anything I regret. It was just that my number one priority, God, became my last priority, and I argued with my parents about having to go to church on Sundays.

The one friendship I value the most would probably surprise most people. I think that most girls who have a sister so close in age would agree with me when I say that even though, when you are young, you fight and try to destroy each other, your sisters are your closest friends. Alina and I have known each other for eleven years and have been sisters for ten. We started off friends in children's church and became stepsisters when our parents married. I didn't like the idea of having her as a sister and found that we argued and fought...and many times I ended up bleeding when she scratched me. I remember one time we fought over the bed, and as we were yelling at each other, scratching and pulling hair, Alina scratched me in the mouth. That happened a few times, and now I just wonder how her hands got in my mouth! As we grew older, I learned to appreciate her more and respect her. I don't know what I would do without her. Alina has always been there for me when I've had problems with school, friends and family. I am so blessed to have such a sister, and I wouldn't swap her for anything. I look out for her, and she looks out for me, and I love her so much. I am so grateful that God has blessed me with such an understanding sister. We still have our moments when we fight, and over some really petty things too, but who doesn't fight with family?

Each and every friendship has a different purpose, and each helps in different stages of our lives. God puts people in your life for a reason, even the bad, because you can learn important lessons from them like trust and how important it is. Friendships are built on three major things: love, trust, and honesty. One without the other destroys a friendship, and these lessons are often learned the hard way. I have learned through other friendships that when someone tells you something, it is best that you keep it to yourself, even if you think that a certain person has the right to know. When the time is right, they can tell that person, and that way no one's trust is broken. Remember that friends shape our future and influence our decisions, so be careful whom you befriend.

you can meet again. And meeting again, after a moment or a lifetime, is certain for those who are friends. Don't be dismayed at good-byes. A farewell is necessary before you can meet again. And meeting again, after a moment or a lifetime, is certain for those who are friends. Don't be dismayed at good-byes. A farewell is necessary before you can meet again. And meeting again, after a moment or a lifetime, is certain for those who are friends. Don't be dismayed at good-byes. A farewell is necessary before you can meet again. And meeting again, after a moment or a lifetime, is certain for those who are friends. Don't be dismayed at good-byes. A farewell is necessary before you can meet again. And meeting again, after a moment or a lifetime, is certain for those who are friends. Don't be dismayed at good-byes. A farewell is necessary before you can meet again. And meeting again, after a moment or a lifetime, is certain for those who are friends. Don't be dismayed at good-byes. A farewell is necessary before you can meet again. And meeting again, after a moment or a lifetime, is certain for those who are friends. Don't be dismayed at good-byes. A farewell is necessary before you can meet again. And meeting again, after a moment or a lifetime, is certain for those who are friends. Don't be dismayed at good-byes. A farewell is necessary before you can meet again. And meeting again, after a moment or a lifetime, is certain for those who are friends. Don't be dismayed at good-byes. A farewell is necessary before you can meet again.

girlfriendship

epilogue: tribute to a friend

"Don't be dismayed at good-byes. A farewell is necessary before you can meet again. And meeting again, after a moment or a lifetime, is certain for those who are friends."
RICHARD BACH

Tribute to a friend
temily's story, age 12

It was probably one of the most exciting days of our lives, our first day of school.

Sinead and I were just normal little five-year-old girls when we first met each other. Who knew we would eventually become such good friends?

I think we were so close because we rarely had arguments. When we did argue, it was normally about the answer to a math problem or the spelling of a word. Schoolwork was one of our shared passions.

As the years went by, our friendship became closer and closer to the point where we could tell each other anything, joke around, and laugh together. Our friendship meant so much to me because it was fun, challenging, exciting....Sinead was just special.

It was just a normal week in fourth grade when I realized that something was very wrong. Sinead hadn't been coming to school for a few days. That afternoon, when I got into the car to go home, my Mom told me everything. She said that we were going to the hospital to visit Sinead. Mom also said that she was really sick and had just been diagnosed with leukemia.

I wasn't quite sure what that meant, but I knew that it was bad, and from that day I was always praying and believing that Sinead would get better, that some day she would be able to live a normal childhood and we could get back to how we were— two good friends having fun together.

When we got to the hospital, Sinead and I started talking, and that was when I realized just how serious her condition was. I sat there feeling completely helpless and wondering why this was happening to my beautiful friend.

Sinead was regularly absent from school, which made the days quite boring. I would always beg Mom to take me to see her so we could catch up, but we couldn't always go. Her immune system was shattered, and any small cough or sore throat would put her in danger. It was best for her to stay away from school, even though that was so hard to do.

Whenever I saw or even thought about Sinead, I would feel frustrated because I couldn't do anything to help her, and the doctors could only do very little. I was also very upset because Sinead's sickness was stopping her from doing the things that she would normally do.

In fifth grade, Sinead had to leave our school to go to a new school where she had been accepted. That felt really bad because we had been together for so long. After she left, we didn't see each other as much anymore. When Sinead's condition eventually got worse, I couldn't see her at all for a while since she had to stay in isolation and wasn't allowed to have visitors.

I remember the last time I saw Sinead. My parents took me to see her at her house. We talked a bit but couldn't converse too much because Sinead was feeling sick and exhausted. I felt really bad as I left because I had come at such a bad time and neither of us could really make the visit worthwhile. When I got home, I cried.

During the hard times, when Sinead wasn't getting better, my friends and I found it quite difficult to be the best friends that we could have possibly been for Sinead. This was partly because, as twelve-year-olds, we had never known this type of thing to happen to someone that we were close to—but also because we didn't know what to do to help her. All we could do was pray.

When I found out that Sinead was in intensive care and was definitely not getting any better, I was terrified—terrified for Sinead and how much she was hurting inside and terrified that I might lose one of my best friends. It was horrible!

It is horrible; I lost one of my best friends. Early one morning, Sinead's mom called to let us know that she had died the night before. There are not really words to describe the feeling I had when I found out. It's still awful, it's still sad.

The following Tuesday was my time to say good-bye. I didn't want to, but the funeral is when you say farewell. I was asked to hand out programs along with some other school friends at the funeral. I've kept one of those programs with her beautiful face on the cover, and I got Mom to press some of the daffodils that were placed on the coffin.

I was also given the opportunity to write a thought that could be read out at Sinead's funeral. I wrote, "Sinead, you looked after one of my best friends, 'Pooh Bear,' and now when I see him, I think of you. You were so good at piano, you made me want to play it too."

As I am writing this and remembering and feeling the loss all over again, I am crying. I miss not being able to e-mail "funnybunny85" or call her up and chat.

I'm grateful for having known Sinead, having had the experiences that we shared, the memories. And even though it was only a little time we had together, I'm thankful to have had that time. I wish I could have spent more time with her. Now I'll just have to wait until I get to heaven. Looking back, I wish I had crammed so much more into the time we had, but I just didn't know it would be so short.

It's not easy, and it's still very sad. She was so special. I miss her so much.

"Some people come into our lives
and quickly go...
Like an ocean wave
When it touches the shore...
Or a cloud that is there
And then gone.
Some people stay for a while,
And although we may be unaware,
They are touching our lives
in a special way.
When they are gone, it is then we
understand...
They have left footprints on our hearts,
And we will never, ever be the same.
That is when we know...
Blessed are we."
FLAVIA WEEDN

P.S.

Every year it seems we get busier and busier. We juggle study, shopping, work, shopping, exercise, shopping, cleaning, and of course...more shopping! It's hard to find time for ourselves, let alone our friends. But deciding to get together with our girlfriends is definitely worth the effort, plus it's a great excuse to let your hair down and have some serious fun.

So we decided to dedicate the next few pages to giving you some advice on things to do and how you can share and celebrate the great times of your life together with the ones that matter.

Enjoy!

All our love,
Mary & Alyson

Tip No.1—Party time

Some of the best times spent together are party times.

Celebrating anything and everything from birthdays, anniversaries, and passing an exam to graduation or getting a new job or promotion are great excuses to throw a bash. In fact, come to think of it, you don't really need an excuse to have a great girlfriendship party!

And the best parties are not with hordes of people you don't know (and those annoying uninvited guests), but with close friends you can have great times and great conversations with.

One of the best parties to throw is a Valentine's Day party, especially if you're single and don't have a particular valentine. Instead of staying at home waiting for that bunch of flowers or anonymous card, why not take the initiative and host a party for all your single friends? It doesn't need to be corny and lovelorn, just well organized and imaginative.

- Have a picnic party and gorge on some yummy gourmet foods, (e.g. chocolate-dipped strawberries, fresh-baked bread and cheese, a selection of antipasto, and of course melt-in-your-mouth chocolate truffles), but ditch the paper plates and plastic cups. Spoil yourselves. Use crystal glasses and quality china.

- Meet in a funky café for breakfast (nothing beats a stack of pancakes or creamy scrambled eggs early in the morning). Organize beforehand so everyone brings a small present for someone else (i.e. candles, bath beads, body lotion) and sweet-talk one of the waiters into handing them out!

- Host a theme dinner party. Get your friends to dress up. Don't sweat it if you can't cook. Just watch some cooking shows or go the cheat's way and order some take-out.

- Arrange a pamper party where you organize someone to come and thoroughly spoil you and your choicest friends with some beauty treatments (i.e. facials, manicures, or pedicures), but beware: This can seriously dent the credit card.

- If none of the above suits your fancy, then organize an oldie but a goody...Chick's Flick Night or movie marathon! Just make sure there's plenty of good friends, comfort food, pillows, and of course, videos or DVDs galore.

Tip No. 2—Golf punks

Don't let the guys have all the fun doing the typical boy sports. Grab some girlfriends and enter the male domain...GOLF!

Golfing is not just a boring weekend pastime for the boys. Some of the best fun to be had is golf-punking on a course. (But ditch the stilettos unless you want to sink your heels instead of the balls.)

If you're beginners, the best way to play is a round of nine holes, Ambrose style.

To play Ambrose golf, you need to form a team of four players (with whom you compete against other teams). At each tee, every player hits her ball, and the one considered to be in the best position is chosen for the next shot. The players pick up and go to the best-placed ball. They then drop their balls within a club length of the original and take their next shot.

The best thing about Ambrose golf is that anyone, regardless of experience, can play and have some fun. Basically, each team has four chances to hit a good shot on every stroke.

If you need more info, the management at your local golf course should be able to help you out by giving you some pointers and letting you know when the next Ambrose tournament is scheduled.

So style up and master those greens. But be warned—golf can be very competitive and very, very addictive!

Tip No. 3—Pizza & piles of cards

If you know anything about the male species, you will have noticed that they, like girls, also enjoy having same-gender get-togethers. The stereotypical guys' night (from what we've seen in the movies and heard in folklore) is made up of pizza, beer, cigars, and poker.

So, we've decided to take the guys' night idea (delete the beer, burping, cigar smoke, and gross-out jokes) and sweeten it with a feminine touch.

Here's the lowdown on how to put together a transformed guys'-into-girls' night:

- Organize with your friends to meet up at a suitable house that has a game-type room and large (preferably round) table.

- Create a moody atmosphere by dimming the lights, lighting some scented candles, and playing a funky CD.

- For the food and drink component, think one word...GOURMET! Ditch the usual bowls of peanuts and pretzels and make up a plate of delectable hors d'oeuvres; forget the tasteless mass-produced pizza and order the scrumptious gourmet variety; forgo the off-brand Neapolitan ice cream and indulge in mini tubs of Italian gelato or sweet strawberry sorbet.

- Now for the cards bit....It's up to you to choose your flavor, but one of the classic card games guaranteed to bring out the worst in you and your friends is called "Cheat." The object of the game is to get rid of all your cards by whatever means necessary. Cheating is, of course, greatly encouraged.

Here are the rules:
- Deal two packs of cards out among all the players.

- Player No. 1 has to put down as many cards of the same value (e.g. a two, a five, a seven, etc.) as she wants to in the center of the table and say what they are (e.g. "two sevens").

- The next player follows by either laying down more cards of the same value or higher or by passing. The point of the game is that the cards are laid facedown and any player can lie about what she has gotten rid of.

- A player can be challenged by any other player to reveal the cards she has just laid down. If a lie has been revealed, then the cheat has to pick up all the cards that have been laid down so far. If, on the other hand, the challenge is incorrect, then the challenger has to pick up the cards.

It's easy to get the hang of the game and see who the good liars and interrogators are. But at the end of the day, it's all a game and a bit of fun...with some yummy pizza thrown in!

Tip No. 4—Hot days and cold cocktails

When the weather heats up and all you want to do is cool down, invite your friends around and treat them to some heavenly ice-cold cocktails (non-alcoholic of course).

All you'll need is a trusty blender (sexy stainless steel ones look the best), tall cocktail glasses, and the theatrical flair of a hip bartender, and you're set. Here are some recipes to get you started:

Tropical Frappe

Ingredients
6 ounces passionfruit juice
2 tablespoons of coconut cream
1 cup pineapple chunks
1 ripe banana
6 large ice cubes

Mix it baby
Combine all ingredients in a blender. Blend until the ice is crushed and the mixture is thick. Serve in tall glasses with straws. Sprinkle ground nutmeg or cinnamon on top and garnish with fresh fruit.

So-You-Can-See-the-Sunrise

Ingredients
4 ounces cranberry juice
2 ½ ounces orange juice
Squeeze of fresh lemon juice
Ginger ale

Mix it baby
Blend the juices with ice until smooth, and pour into a tall glass. Top with a splash of ginger ale. Garnish with strawberries, and serve with a straw.

Smooth Groover

Ingredients

3 ounches ginger ale
½ ripe banana
2 cups of strawberries
1 tablespoon of sugar
4-ounce scoop of vanilla ice cream

Mix it baby

Mix all ingredients in a blender. Garnish with halved strawberries and a cocktail umbrella.

Tip No. 5—Angels and mortals

Okay, so you and your friends saw the *Charlie's Angels* movies and thought to yourselves, "We'll definitely have what they're having." Starring those gorgeous gals— Drew Barrymore, Lucy Lui, and Cameron Diaz—*Charlies Angel's 1 & 2* showed us that girls can be funny, smart, outrageous, and kick some serious butt in sky-high stilettos (but didn't we know that all along?).

So here are two of the best full-throttle activities you and your friends can make a weekend of:

Surfing Sistas

For those near the beach, surfing is a great sport to do with your girlfriends, and the exhilarating rush you get from catching a wave is incredible, but it is one of the toughest sports to master. So before you go out and buy that board and bikini, it's worth you and your girlfriends getting some proper lessons. Also, you'll be competing for the waves with guys, who can be intimidating and not take too kindly to some chicks surfing their turf, so the lessons will help you gain some confidence.

Another thing to remember is to make sure you can actually swim! Yes, that's right, knowing how to swim in the wet blue yonder is an important prerequisite for Surfing 101. And don't even think about using your surfboard as a pool lounge; that's not what it's for. Remember, surfing with floaties or a lifejacket is not a cool look!

Dirt-bike Divas

If you want to get down and dirty, there are plenty of dirt-bike tracks and bikes for hire. Grab your girlfriends and get into your old jeans, well-worn jackets, and tennis shoes, but ditch the Angels-style drag queen makeup.

Here are some tips to start your engines with:
- Always wear a helmet and the right safety gear.
- Start on a bike that you are comfortable with, even if it may not be a "cool" one. Remember you're riding to simply have a bit of fun.

- Balance is important. To stop you from falling off, you have to counterbalance the bike. When you're going around bends and turns, lean yourself into the bike, and if you're going up a hill, lean forward.

- If you're unfamiliar with this sport, be prepared to be very, very sore. So stock up on the Epsom salts and have a good tub soak afterward to ease those muscles.

Tip No. 6—Road trip

Ahhh, the romance of a road trip. Driving into the horizon in a classic convertible with your girlfriends and singing along to the *Best of Abba* ("Dancing Queen" was always our fave) with the wind blowing your just-stepped-out-of-a-salon-look hair.

Whether you want to take a day trip or spend a few days coming of age in your car, a road trip with your girlfriends is definitely one of the best experiences you can have. But to avoid a road trip disaster, you need to prepare well and pay attention to the little details.

- Before you head out, make sure that your car has been recently serviced and that you have a full tank of fuel. Breaking down in the middle of nowhere is no fun and will only remind you of every B-grade urban myth movie you've ever seen.

- Don't be ignorant of basic car care. It's important to know how to change a flat or blown tire and check the oil and coolant. You don't want to be dependant on passing motorists to help you with simple stuff you should already know.

- Keep a road map in the car and master the art of reading it. Nothing spoils a road trip more than being lost and not knowing how to get to where you want to go. Plus, knowing how to read a road map will definitely impress the present or future guy in your life and will prevent many in-car quarrels!

- Regularly change drivers to avoid driver fatigue, and have frequent rest stops.

- If you plan to stay overnight somewhere, it's good to check ahead to see if there are available accommodations. It's fun driving in your car, but you don't want to have to sleep in it too!

- Stop to smell the roses in the towns you pass. Don't rush the road trip. Stop, savor, and enjoy the passing towns!

- Capture the moment by taking some classic Polaroids, or better yet, videotape the trip and have a memorable keepsake.

- Take a selection of favorite CDs. Nothing creates the right mood like great music.

- Take along some easy-to-eat nibbles, and depending upon the weather, some iced coffees or hot chocolates to drink.

- Remember it's not the destination that's important but the journey along the way. So take your time and connect with your girlfriends.

Tip No. 7—Buff and beautiful

Exercise should be a regular part of your lifestyle. It keeps you fit and healthy, clears your mind, gets rid of all those nasty toxins, and releases endorphins that give you a safe and natural high. But staying committed to regularly exercising can be hard—unless you have an exercise buddy.

Exercising with a friend is a sure way to keep you faithful to your New Year's resolution of being buff and beautiful. On the days you don't feel like treading the treadmill or pounding the pavement, she can encourage and hold you accountable to your commitment, and vice versa.

So, now the hard decision is what to do. Here are some suggestions:

- Get a gym membership together. Many gyms now offer two-for-one memberships, saving you a ton of money.
- Go biking and burn those butts.
- Swimming is a great low-impact alternative (although seeing some guys in Speedos might turn you off).
- Boxing, kickboxing, and aeroboxing are all great comprehensive workouts and good ways to get rid of all that pent-up frustration.
- Walking and running are free and easy.
- Surfing.
- Pilates. It's low-impact and quickly becoming one of the most popular exercise choices.
- Dancing.
- Horseback riding.
- Aerobics.

Remember, choose something that you both enjoy and can commit to.

Tip No. 8—Window-shop till you drop

We're positive that when God created the female species, He embedded something in our genetic makeup that was predisposed to a particular pastime...SHOPPING!

Nothing seems to get us quite as excited as the S-word, and when we combine shopping and hanging out with our friends, it seems as if all our Christmases have come at once.

But shopping can also be expensive. Yes, it's sad but true. So to avoid the credit card blues, why not spend a day simply window-shopping instead? You'll be surprised how satisfying it can be. In fact, we have a theory that the joy is found in being in the shops, not just in the spending (but we have yet to prove that theory).

Start the day with a leisurely sleep-in, and meet your girlfriend for brunch at your favorite café. Then go to the city's *très chic* shopping center and browse, browse, browse. Let your senses go into overdrive, and touch, smell, and try on as much as you can.

Make sure you recharge midafternoon by stopping to have a caffeine and muffin/donut/pastry break. If you desperately cannot shop without being tempted to buy something, then set yourself a small limit and stick to it. You'll be surprised—if you look for a bargain, you can find it.

Try to remember that you don't always need to spend a lot of money to have a good time. Good friends, good browsing, and good coffee are sometimes all you need.

Tip No. 9—
Knit and purl

One of the biggest trends to hit the hip and fashionable A-list set is knitting. Yes, that's right, knitting, the customary pastime of grannies worldwide has now become the IN thing for the IT people to do.

Celebrities who are proud to knit are Cameron Diaz, Julia Roberts, and Sandra Bullock. Even the gladiator himself, Russell Crowe, is apparently a happy stress-free knitter. And popping up all over in places such as the USA, Australia, Japan, and the UK are knitting clubs, where the devoted meet to click their cares away.

Knitting has also been touted as the "new yoga" because of its calming benefits (although don't expect to get a body like Gwyneth), and because it lowers your blood pressure (great for exam time) and teaches you patience (especially when you get your first snag).

But by far the best thing about knitting (apart from making must-have hand-knit scarves) is that you can enjoy it with your friends and do it just about anywhere. You and your friends can be knitting buddies at the beach, on the train, on the bus, at the park, and at home. And while getting your regular fabric fix, you can have a great chat too!

So, what are you waiting for? Knit and purl with the girls and enjoy the hobby du jour of the celebrity set.

Tip No. 10—
Regular rituals

We've saved the most important tip until last: remembering to spend time with each other by creating regular rituals. This is where you schedule to do something with your friend on a daily, weekly, monthly, or yearly basis. Here are some ideas:

Daily
- Phone each other
- Send an e-mail
- Exercise together
- Send a text message

Weekly
- Catch up for coffee
- Meet up for breakfast, brunch, or lunch
- Hang out at the beach, park, or one of your houses
- Meet to watch your fave television show

Monthly
- Get a manicure together
- Have an ultimate girls' night
- Go out for dinner
- Watch a movie
- Have a picnic

Yearly
- Take a vacation together
- Go on a road trip
- Rough it and go camping
- Celebrate each other's birthdays
- Celebrate special holidays and anniversaries together

So what are you waiting for? Make time for each other, create those special rituals, and enjoy the journey of girlfriendship!

"Let the soul be assured that somewhere in the universe it should rejoin its friend, and it would be content and cheerful alone for a thousand years."

RALPH WALDO EMERSON

Endnotes

1.   Stambler, L., "Plucked from the Jaws," *Who Weekly* (Milsons Point NSW: February 2004).
2.   Ibid.
3.   Oakes-Ash, R., *Anything She Can Do I Can Do Better* (Milsons Point, NSW: Random House Australia Pty Ltd, 2003).

girlfriendship CD
a companion CD to *girlfriendship*

From the little girl playing dress-up with her sister to the sixteen year old staying up late to talk with her friends on the phone, one thing is constant: the need to share. We are social creatures, and this is nowhere more apparent than in the realm of "girlhood." A girl's experiences are meant to be shared with others. In this companion CD to Mary Simpson and Alyson Passauer's book *girlfriendship*, Kate Miner, Nikki Fletcher, Amy Buckle, and several other female vocalists invite girls and young women to share in a powerful, musical, and exciting worship experience.

UPC: 6-30809-68981-0 • ISBN: 0-88368-891-3 • CD

www.whitakerhouse.com

www.deepercalling.com

Maybe Sunday
by *Britta Adams*

Christian pop sensation Britta is on the scene.
This soulful album is replete with rich sounds critics
are likening to the unique style of Tracy Chapman
and folk rocker Carole King. Raised in a strongly musical family,
Adams' undeniable love for music was evident early in her life.
Maybe Sunday is her debut album.

UPC: 6-30809-68925-2 • ISBN: 0-88368-925-1 • CD

www.whitakerhouse.com

www.deepercalling.com